Saints

for
young readers
for every day

Second Edition
Volume 1
January–June

Revised and Edited by
Susan Helen Wallace, fsp

Illustrated by
Jamie H. Aven

BOOKS & MEDIA
BOSTON

Library of Congress-in-Publication Data

Saints for young readers for every day / revised and edited
   by Susan Helen Wallace. — 2nd ed.
         p.   cm.
   Includes indexes.
      ISBN 0-8198-6970-8 (set : hardcover). — ISBN 0-8198-
6971-6 (set : pbk.). — ISBN 0-8198-6966-X (v. 1 : hardcover).
— ISBN 0-8198-6967-8 (v. 1 pbk.). — ISBN 0-8198-6968-6
(v. 2 : hardcover). — ISBN 0-8198-6969-4 (v. 2 : pbk.).
   1. Christian saints—Biography—Juvenile literature.
[1. Saints.]   I. Wallace, Susan Helen, 1940-
BX4653.D34   1994
282' .092'2—dc20
[B]   94-11927
                                                         CIP
                                                          AC

Cover Illustration by Elinor Kaslow

Printed and published in the U.S.A. by Pauline Books & Media, 50
St. Paul's Avenue, Boston, MA 02130.

http://www.pauline.org   E-mail: PBM_EDIT@INTERRAMP.COM

Pauline Books & Media is the publishing house of the Daughters of
St. Paul, an international congregation of women religious serving
the Church with the communications media.

2 3 4 5 6 7 8 9 10   06 05 04 03 02 01 00 99 98 97

*"I will make a little progress in virtue
every day until death."*

Dedicated to
Venerable Maggiorino Vigolungo

Maggiorino was a teenager of our times who reached a hero's level of love for God and people by following his challenging slogan:

"Make a little progress every day."

Known as the young apostle of the press, Maggiorino joined the newly established Society of St. Paul in his native Italy. His burning ideal shines clearly in his own words: "With the help of God, I intend to consecrate my entire life to spreading the message of Christ through the apostolate of the media. I want to become a saint, a great saint—and soon!"

God willed that Maggiorino would have a short life on this earth. He was just fourteen when he died, but he was ready. In fact, he had written, "Heaven! Eternal happiness! This is what is waiting for me."

How to Use this Book

This book offers stories of saints. Some lived long lives; others died when they were young. Some were close to God from childhood and teen-age years. Others learned the hard way that only God can make us happy.

You will meet saints from every nation and race. They are from different centuries, starting with the early days of the Church, right down to our own times. You will come to know saintly kings and laborers, queens and housemaids, popes and priests, nuns and religious brothers. They were mothers and fathers, teenagers and children. They were doctors and farmers, soldiers and lawyers.

Saints were as different from each other as we are. They were as human as we are. They lived on this earth, experienced temptations and faced problems. They became saints because they used their will power to make right choices and they prayed. They tried to correct their faults and they never gave up trusting in Jesus' love for them.

What is the best way to read this book? First of all, do not try to read all the stories in a few days. Read the saints a day at a time. Most days have one saint to think about. A few days have two or three.

For example, the new Roman calendar offers three saints on May 25 and June 22. We have done the same here. The new calendar offers St. Frances of Rome on March 9. We present her story and then add St. Dominic Savio from an older Church calendar. We did this because the book is for children and Dominic became a saint while young.

The saint for the day is the saint from the current Roman calendar. When the calendar does not present a saint that day, we have gone to the previous calendar and have chosen a saint or blessed we thought you might appreciate knowing. The saints and blesseds for North America are also included here.

You might ask: what is the difference between a SAINT and a BLESSED? Saints are holy persons now in heaven who grew close to God while on earth. The Church declares them saints so that we can love, imitate and pray to them. Saints can pray to God for us and help us. Persons declared BLESSED are holy people who are now in heaven. Usually the Church requires miracles obtained through their intervention. When the miracles have been carefully studied and accepted as real, the blesseds are proclaimed saints. You will also meet MARTYRS in this book. Martyrs allowed themselves to be put to death rather than give up the Catholic faith.

Keep these true stories by your bedside and read the saint of the day before or after morning or evening prayers. In this way, you will be able to think about what you read throughout the day. Read also the brief recommendation at the end of each biography. Try to practice that suggestion. Slowly but surely you will see an improvement in yourself. And there is no telling where you may go from there. Maybe you, too, will become a saint. And why not?

Here is a friendly tip: if you find it hard to be the kind of person you want to be, why not ask the saint of that day to help you? By the end of the year you will have many wonderful friends. You might also want to read more biographies about the saints you especially liked.

CONTENTS

January

ſEBRUARY

march

april

may

June

For an alphabetical listing of the all the saints and blesseds in volumes one and two, see page 332.

January

JANUARY 1

MARY, MOTHER OF GOD

Remember on Christmas morning how we found our way to the stable? It may have been the stable on the mantle or under the Christmas tree or in our parish church. We gazed at the baby in the manger just like the shepherds had done so long ago. Jesus was there with Mary and Joseph. Today we begin our new year at the Eucharistic Celebration. We thank God for Mary, Jesus' mother, who brought the Savior into the world. Because she is the mother of Jesus, God's Son, she truly is the Mother of God. Through the power of the Holy Spirit, Mary conceived Jesus. Joseph was Jesus' loving foster-father.

God chose Mary to be the mother of his Son. She was a teenager and her parents were Joachim and Anne. Mary loved God and her Jewish religion. She was probably considered ordinary by her neighbors. It would be God's work in her that would make her so special, so blessed. God sent the Archangel Gabriel to Mary's town of Nazareth. The angel asked her to accept a wonderful plan—wonderful for her and for all of us. Mary wanted to please God and she accepted the plan.

She became Jesus' mother. Mary and her husband, Joseph, tried to raise Jesus the best way they could and with great love. Jesus spent many happy, quiet years with Mary and Joseph in Nazareth.

When Jesus was about thirty years old, he began his preaching and healing ministry. This is usually called his public life. It seems that sometime before that Joseph had died. Jesus could not now stay just in the little home and carpenter shop at Nazareth. Mary frequently went with her friends to be near her Son. Mary attended a marriage celebration in Cana. Jesus and his disciples came too. When the wine was gone, Mary asked Jesus to do something. She wanted him to save the couple from being embarrassed in front of their guests. He worked the miracle of turning plain water into delicious wine. Mary loved Jesus and believed in him. She was there when he was nailed to the cross. In fact, she stayed right beneath the cross and received his dead body into her arms. After the resurrection, Mary waited with Jesus' apostles for the coming of the Holy Spirit on Pentecost. The apostles loved her. They knew they needed more courage to be real followers of Jesus. Mary prayed for them and encouraged them. She taught them how to be disciples of her Son. Mary's feast days are special events that happen throughout the year. Today's feast honors her as God's Mother. She wants to be our mother, too.

On this first day of the year, we ask Mary to always be there for us as she was for Jesus and his followers.

ST. BASIL AND ST. GREGORY NAZIANZEN

Basil and Gregory were born in Asia Minor in the year 330. This area is modern-day Turkey. Basil's grandmother, father, mother, two brothers and a sister are all saints. Gregory's parents are St. Nonna and St. Gregory the Elder. Basil and Gregory met and became great friends at school in Athens, Greece.

Basil became a well-known teacher. One day his sister, St. Macrina, suggested that he become a monk. He listened to her advice, moved to the wilderness and there started his first monastery. The rule he gave his monks was very wise. Monasteries in the East have followed it down to our own times.

Both Basil and Gregory became priests and then bishops. They preached bravely against the Arian heresy which denied that Jesus is God. This heresy was confusing people.

While he was bishop of Constantinople, Gregory converted many people with his wonderful preaching. This nearly cost him his life. A young man planned to murder him. He repented at the last moment and begged Gregory's forgiveness. Gregory did forgive him and won him with his gentle goodness.

Forty-four of Gregory's speeches, 243 letters and many poems were published. His writings are still important today. Many writers have based their works on his.

Gregory's friend Basil had a very kind and generous heart. He always found time to help the poor. He even invited people who were poor themselves to help those worse off. "Give your last loaf to the beggar at your door," he urged, "and trust in God's goodness." He gave away his inheritance and opened a soup kitchen where he could often be seen wearing an apron and feeding the hungry.

Basil died in 379 at the age of forty-nine. Gregory died in 390 at the age of sixty. He is buried in St. Peter's Basilica in Rome.

We will never be sorry for using our education, time and talents to help the people around us become closer to God.

❧

JANUARY 3

ST. GENEVIEVE

Genevieve was born around 422 in Nanterre, a small village four miles from Paris. While still very young, she desired to devote her life to Jesus. After her parents died, Genevieve went to live with her grandmother. She spent time praying every day. She became very close to Jesus and wanted to bring his goodness to people. Genevieve was a kind, generous person. She went out of her way to do good things for others.

The people of Paris were going to run away from a terrible army coming to attack them. Genevieve stepped forward. She encouraged the citizens to trust in God. She said that if they did penance, they would be spared. The people did what she said, and the fierce army of Huns suddenly turned back. They did not attack the city at all.

St. Genevieve practiced charity and obedience to God's will every day of her life, not just in times of need. She never gave up trying to do as much good as possible. Faithfulness to Jesus and courage are the special gifts of witness she leaves for us.

One of the best ways for us to help our country is to pray for our leaders. We should ask God to guide them for the good of us all.

JANUARY 4

ST. ELIZABETH ANN SETON

"Mother Seton" was the name everyone knew her by when she died on January 4, 1821, in Emmitsburg, Maryland. A life full of surprises had led to that name.

Elizabeth was born in New York City on August 28, 1774. Her father, Richard Bayley, was a

well-known doctor. Her mother, Catherine, died when Elizabeth was very young. Elizabeth was Episcopalian. As a teenager, she did many things to help poor people.

In 1794, Elizabeth married William Seton. He was a rich merchant who owned a fleet of ships. Elizabeth, William and their five children had a happy life together. But suddenly William lost his fortune and his good health within a short time. His wife heard that the weather in Italy might help him get better. Elizabeth, William and their oldest daughter, Anna, journeyed there by ship. But William died shortly after. Elizabeth and Anna remained in Italy as guests of the Filicchi family. The Filicchis were very kind. They tried to make Elizabeth and Anna's sorrow easier by sharing their own deep love for the Catholic faith. Elizabeth returned home to New York convinced she would become a Catholic. Her family and friends did not understand. They were very upset, but she went ahead with courage. Elizabeth joined the Church on March 4, 1805.

A few years later, Elizabeth was asked to come and open a girls' school in Baltimore. It was there that Elizabeth decided to live as a sister. Many women came to join her, including her sister and sister-in-law. Her own daughters, Anna and Catherine, also joined the group. They became the American Sisters of Charity and Elizabeth was given the title "Mother Seton." Elizabeth became well-known. She started many Catholic schools and a few orphanages. She made plans for a hospital which was opened after her death. Elizabeth loved to write, and she also translated some textbooks from French to English. But she was most famous for the way she visited the poor and the sick.

Elizabeth was declared a saint by Pope Paul VI on September 14, 1975.

If something should happen that changes our lives from happy to difficult, let us turn to God as Mother Seton did and ask for help. God can help us see how hard things can bring out our hidden talents. Then we will accomplish what we never dreamed of.

JANUARY 5

ST. JOHN NEUMANN

Not only was John Neumann quiet, he was short—five feet, two inches tall. His eyes were very kind and he smiled a lot. He was born on March 28, 1811, in Bohemia, now part of the Czech Republic. His parents were Philip and Agnes Neumann. He had four sisters and a brother. After college, John entered the seminary. When time came for ordination, the bishop was sick. The date was never set because Bohemia had enough priests at the time. Since he had been reading about missionary activities in the United States, John decided to go to America to ask for ordination. He walked most of the way to France and then boarded the ship *Europa*.

John arrived in Manhattan on June 9, 1836. Bishop John Dubois was very happy to see him. There were only thirty-six priests for the two hundred thousand Catholics living in the state of New York and part of New Jersey. Just sixteen days after his arrival, John was ordained a priest and sent to Buffalo. There he would help Father Pax care for his parish, which was nine hundred square miles in size. Father Pax gave him the choice of the city of Buffalo or of the country area. Now John's heroic character began to show. He chose the most difficult—the country area. He decided to stay in a little town with an unfinished church. Once it was completed, he moved to another town that had a log-church. There he built himself a small log cabin. He hardly ever lit a fire and often lived on bread and water. He only slept a few hours each night. The farms in his area were far apart. John had to walk long distances to reach his people. They were German, French, Irish and Scotch. In school, John had learned eight languages. Now he added English and Gaelic. Before he died, he knew twelve languages.

John joined the Redemptorist order and continued his missionary work. He became bishop of Philadelphia in 1852. Bishop Neumann built fifty churches and began building a cathedral. He opened almost one hundred schools, and the number of parochial school students grew from five hundred to nine thousand. Bishop Neumann's health never improved much, but people were still

very surprised when he died suddenly on January 5, 1860. He was walking home from an appointment when he fell to the ground with a stroke. He was carried into the nearest house and died there at 3:00 P.M. In March Bishop Neumann would have been forty-nine. He was proclaimed a saint by Pope Paul VI on June 19, 1977.

We might not be as smart, strong, or active as we would like to be. But that doesn't stop God from loving us and from using us to do wonderful things. When we have to do something difficult, we can ask St. John Neumann's help.

JANUARY 6

BLESSED ANDRE BESSETTE

Alfred Bessette was born on August 9, 1845, not far from Montreal, Canada. He was the eighth of twelve children. When Alfred was nine, his father, a wood cutter, died in an accident at work. Three years later, Alfred's mother died of tuberculosis, leaving the children orphans. They were split up and placed in different homes. Alfred went to live with his aunt and uncle.

Because his family had been so poor and he was often sick, Alfred had very little education. So for the next thirteen years he tried learning different trades like farming, shoemaking and baking.

He even worked in a factory in Connecticut. But his health always failed him.

When Alfred was twenty-five, he joined the order of Holy Cross and chose the name Brother Andre. He spent the next forty years as a general maintenance man and messenger. The remaining years of his life were spent as the doorkeeper for the order's college. Here, Brother Andre's healing power became known. When people came to ask him for a cure, he would tell them to first thank God for their suffering because it was so valuable. Then he would pray with them. Most of them were cured. Brother Andre always refused credit for the healing. He insisted it had been the person's faith and the power of St. Joseph.

Brother Andre had a great love for the Eucharist and for St. Joseph. When he was young, he dreamt he saw a big church, but he couldn't tell where it was. Gradually, he came to realize that God wanted a church in honor of St. Joseph. That church was to be built on top of Mount Royale in Montreal, Canada. Prayer and the sacrifices of Brother Andre and many other people made the dream come true. The magnificent church honoring St. Joseph was built. It is a testimony to Brother Andre's tremendous faith. Pilgrims come to Mount Royale all year and from distant places. They want to honor St. Joseph. They want to show their trust in his loving care, as Brother Andre did.

Brother Andre died peacefully on January 6, 1937. Nearly a million people climbed Mount Royale to St. Joseph's Oratory for his funeral. They came in spite of sleet and snow to say goodbye to their dear friend. He was proclaimed "blessed" on May 23, 1982, by Pope John Paul II.

We can profit by the examples and help of the great St. Joseph, as Brother Andre did. St. Joseph and Blessed Andre will help us know how to be good friends of Jesus. Let us ask them often to help us.

JANUARY 7

ST. RAYMOND OF PENYAFORT

Raymond was born between 1175 and 1180 in a little town near Barcelona, Spain. He was educated at the cathedral school in Barcelona and became a priest. Raymond graduated from law school in Bologna, Italy, and became a famous teacher. He joined the Dominican order in 1218. In 1230, Pope Gregory IX asked this dedicated priest to come to Rome. When Raymond arrived, the pope gave him several assignments. One duty was to collect all the official letters of the popes since 1150. Raymond gathered and published five volumes. He also took part in writing Church law.

In 1238, Raymond was elected master general of the Dominicans. With his knowledge of law, he went over the order's rule and made sure everything was legally correct. After he had finished, he resigned his position in 1240. Now he could truly dedicate the rest of his life to parish work. That is what he really wanted.

The pope thought of making Raymond an archbishop, but Raymond refused. He asked to return to Spain and he did. He was overjoyed to be in parish work. His compassion helped many people return to God through the sacrament of Reconciliation.

During his years in Rome, Raymond had often heard stories of the difficulties that missionaries were having. They were trying hard to reach out to the non-Christians of Northern Africa and Spain. To help the missionaries, Raymond started a school that taught the language and culture of the people to be evangelized. Also, Father Raymond asked the famous Dominican, St. Thomas Aquinas, to write a booklet. This booklet would explain the truths of faith in a way that nonbelievers could understand. (We celebrate the feast of St. Thomas on January 28.)

Raymond lived nearly one hundred years. He died in Barcelona on January 6, 1275. He was proclaimed a saint in 1601 by Pope Clement VIII. This pope declared him the patron of Church lawyers because of his great influence on Church law.

Raymond could never have done so much in his life without his love for prayer and for the Blessed Mother. When we are asked to do many things, let us turn to Our Lady and ask her help.

JANUARY 8
ST. THORFINN

The details of St. Thorfinn's life were discovered long after his death. He died in 1285, in a monastery in Belgium. Fifty years later, his tomb was accidentally opened during some construction work. Everyone was surprised by the strong, pleasant smell that came out of his coffin. The abbot started investigating. He found one elderly monk, Walter de Muda, who remembered Thorfinn. In fact, Father Walter had been so impressed with Thorfinn's gentle goodness and firmness, that he had written a poem about him. Walter had placed the poem with Thorfinn in the tomb. The monks went to look for the poem. They found the parchment just as new and fresh as the day it had been put there.

The monks felt this was a sign that God wanted Thorfinn to be remembered and honored. People started praying to him and miracles began to happen. Father Walter was asked to write whatever he could remember about Thorfinn. He wrote that Thorfinn had come from Norway. As a priest he probably had served at the cathedral. It seems that Thorfinn had signed an important document while at the cathedral. He had been a witness to the Agreement of Tonsberg in 1277. This agreement between King Magnus VI and the archbishop freed the Church from state control. But a few years later, King Eric rejected the agreement. He turned against the archbishop and those who had supported him. The archbishop was sent away and so was Thorfinn, who was now bishop of Hamar, Norway.

Thorfinn started a hard journey to Flanders. He was even shipwrecked on the trip. Finally, he arrived and went to live at the monastery where he later died. He visited Rome, but he returned very ill. Thorfinn didn't have much, but he divided a few possessions among his family members and some charitable groups. Then he died on January 8, 1285. The Catholics in Hamar, Norway, still honor St. Thorfinn and celebrate his feast day.

Sometimes it might seem that good people are overlooked and are not appreciated. If we ever feel that way about ourselves or someone we love, we can pray to St. Thorfinn. He will help us see that what really counts is to be important to God.

JANUARY 9

ST. JULIAN AND ST. BASILISSA

St. Julian and St. Basilissa were husband and wife. They lived in the early part of the fourth century. Their love for their faith led them to do something heroic: they turned their home into a hospital. This way, they could take care of the sick and the poor who had no one to help them.

St. Julian took care of the men, and St. Basilissa cared for the women. The couple found Jesus in the people they served. And they did what they did because of love, not for money or any kind of reward.

We do not have many details about the day-to-day life of this couple. We do know, however, that St. Basilissa died after suffering great persecutions for the faith. Julian lived much longer. He continued his generous service to sick people even after Basilissa had died. Later, Julian, too, died a martyr.

Basilissa and Julian spent their whole lives helping others and serving God. They planted the seed of faith by living in a holy way. They watered that faith and made it grow with their blood shed for Jesus crucified.

We can imitate these saints by visiting sick or lonely people. We can cheer them up and be good listeners, too.

❧

JANUARY 10

ST. WILLIAM

St. William came from a wealthy French family. Even as a boy, he did not waste time fooling around or being idle. He spent time praying every day. When he joined the Cistercian order, he tried to be a good monk. His fellow monks admired him, even though he was not trying to impress anybody.

St. William had a great devotion to Jesus in the Blessed Sacrament. He practiced penance without showing how hard it was. He always seemed to be happy. When he was made abbot of the community, he remained humble. He was just himself. When the archbishop of Bourges died, William was chosen to take his place. He was grateful to be consecrated a bishop, but unhappy because of all the attention he would receive. He kept humble by performing penances for his own soul and for the conversion of sinners.

Although William loved to be alone with God in the Blessed Sacrament, he knew it was his duty as archbishop to travel all over his diocese willingly. He celebrated the Eucharist and preached the faith. He visited the poor and sick, to console them and bring them to Christ.

Archbishop William died on January 10, 1209. He was buried in the cathedral of Bourges. Miracles were reported by people who prayed at his tomb. William was proclaimed a saint in 1218 by Pope Honorius III.

The more we read about the saints, the more we realize how they became saints. They prayed, obeyed, were self-sacrificing, and trusted in God.

JANUARY 11

ST. THEODOSIUS

Theodosius was born in Asia Minor in 423. As a young man, he set out on pilgrimage to the Holy Land. People say he was inspired by Abraham's journey of faith recorded in the Bible's book of Genesis.

After visiting the holy places, he decided to lead a life of prayer. He asked the guidance of a holy man named Longinus. Soon people realized how holy Theodosius himself was. Many men asked to join him. They, too, wanted to be monks.

Theodosius built a large monastery at Cathismus, near Bethlehem. Before long, it was filled with monks from Greece, Armenia, Arabia, Persia and the Slavic countries. Eventually, it grew into a "little city." One building was for sick people, one for the elderly and one for the poor and homeless.

Theodosius was always generous. He fed an endless stream of poor people. Sometimes it seemed like there would not be enough food for the monks. But Theodosius had great trust in God. He never turned travelers away, even when food was scarce. The monastery was a very peaceful place. The monks lived in silence and prayer. It was going so well that the patriarch of Jerusalem appointed Theodosius head of all the monks in the east.

Theodosius died in 529 at the age of 106. The

patriarch of Jerusalem and many people attended his funeral. Theodosius was buried where he had first lived as a monk. It was called the Cave of the Magi. The cave received its name from people who believed that the Wise Men had stayed there when they came in search of Jesus.

Let us try, as Theodosius did, to get closer to God in our everyday life. God will give us the courage we need.

❧

ST. MARGUERITE BOURGEOYS

Marguerite was born in Troyes, France, on April 17, 1620, but spent most of her eighty years in Montreal, Canada. Marguerite was the sixth of twelve children. Her parents were devout people. When Marguerite was nineteen, her mother died. Marguerite took care of her younger brothers and sisters. Her father died when she was twenty-seven. The family was now raised and Marguerite prayed to know what to do with her life. The governor of Montreal, Canada, was visiting France. He tried to find teachers for the New World. He invited Marguerite to come to Montreal to teach school and religion classes. She said yes.

Marguerite gave away her share of her parents' inheritance to other members of the family. They couldn't believe that she would really leave their civilized country to go to the wilderness an ocean away. But she did. She sailed on June 20, 1653, and arrived in Canada in mid-November. Marguerite began the construction of a chapel in 1657. It was to honor Our Lady of Good Help. In 1658, she opened her first school. Marguerite realized the need to recruit more teachers. She returned to France in 1659 and returned with four companions. In 1670, she went to France again and brought back six companions. These brave women became the first sisters of the Congregation of Notre Dame.

St. Marguerite and her sisters helped people in the colony survive when food was scarce. They opened a vocational school and taught young people how to run a home and farm. St. Marguerite's congregation was growing. By 1681 there were eighteen sisters. Seven were Canadian. They opened more missions and two sisters taught at the Indian mission. St. Marguerite herself received the first two Indian women into the congregation.

In 1693, Mother Marguerite handed over her congregation to her successor. The new superior was Marie Barbier, the first Canadian to join the order. St. Marguerite's religious rule was approved by the Church in 1698. Marguerite spent her last few years praying and writing an autobiography. On the last day of 1699, a young sister lay dying. Mother Marguerite asked the Lord to take her life in exchange. By the morning of January 1, 1700, the sister was completely well. Mother Marguerite had a raging fever. She suffered for twelve days and died on January 12, 1700. She was declared a saint by Pope John Paul II on April 2, 1982.

When we don't have enough courage to do good things, we can ask St. Marguerite Bourgeoys to make us brave and generous like her.

❧

JANUARY 13

ST. HILARY OF POITIERS

In the early centuries of Christianity, there were still many people who did not believe in God as we do. They believed that there were many gods, some more powerful than others. These people were not bad. They just did not know any better. They were called pagans.

In the year 315, Hilary was born into just such a family in Poitiers, a town in France. His family was rich and well-known. Hilary received a good education. He married and raised a family.

Through his studies, Hilary learned that a person should practice patience, kindness, justice and as many good habits as possible. These good acts would be rewarded in the life after death. Hilary's studies also convinced him that there could only be one God who is eternal, all-powerful and good. He read the Bible for the first time. When he came to the story of Moses and the burning bush, Hilary was very impressed by the name God gave himself: I AM WHO AM. Hilary read the writings of the prophets, too. Then he read the whole New Testament. By the time he finished, he was completely converted to Christianity and was baptized.

Hilary lived the faith so well that he was appointed a bishop. This did not make his life easy because the emperor was interfering in Church matters. When Hilary opposed him, the emperor exiled him. And here is where Hilary's great virtues of patience and courage shone. He accepted exile calmly and used the time to write books explaining the faith.

Since he was becoming famous, Hilary's enemies asked the emperor to send him back to his hometown. There he would be less noticeable. So Hilary returned to Poitiers in 360. He continued writing and teaching the people about the faith. Hilary died eight years later, at the age of fifty-two. His books have influenced the Church right to our own day. That is why he is called a Doctor of the Church.

No one's life is easy. But as we learn from Hilary, it is not so much what happens in our life that matters, as what we do with what happens.

JANUARY 14

ST. MACRINA

On January 2, we celebrated the feast of a grandchild of today's saint. St. Basil the Great, who was born around 329, came from a family of saints. Macrina, his father's mother, was one of his favorites. She seems to have raised Basil. As an adult, he praised his grandmother for all the good she had done for him. He especially thanked her openly for having taught him to love the Christian faith from the time he was very small.

Macrina and her husband learned the high price of being true to their Christian beliefs. During one of the Roman persecutions of Galerius and Maximinus, Basil's grandparents were forced into hiding. They found refuge in the forest near their home. Somehow they managed to escape their persecutors. They were always hungry and afraid, but they would not give up their faith. Instead, they patiently waited and prayed for the persecution to end. They hunted for food and ate the wild vegetation and somehow survived. This persecution lasted seven years. St. Gregory Nazianzen, who shares Basil's feast day on January 2, recorded these few details.

During another persecution, Macrina and her husband had all their property and belongings taken from them. They were left with nothing but their faith and trust in God's care for them.

St. Macrina survived her husband but the exact year of each of their deaths is not recorded. It is believed that Macrina died around 340. Her grandchild, Basil, died in 379.

St. Macrina was a loving grandmother. She made Christianity beautiful to Basil and the rest of her family because she really lived what she talked about. We can ask St. Macrina to help us be the same kind of Christian she was.

JANUARY 15

ST. PAUL THE HERMIT

When St. Paul died at the age of 113, he had a long life to look back on. It must have given him much joy and peace at the moment of his death. This is why:

Paul was born into a Christian family in the year 229. They lived in Thebes, Egypt. Paul's parents showed him by their own lives how to love God and worship him with one's whole heart. Paul was certainly very sad to lose both his parents when he was just fifteen years old.

A few years later, in 250, Emperor Decius started a cruel persecution of the Church. Paul hid in his friend's home, but he still was not safe. His brother-in-law was after his money and property. The man could easily betray him to the authorities.

So Paul fled to the desert. He found a cave near a palm tree and a spring of fresh water. There he settled. He sewed palm branches together for clothes, and he lived on fruit and water.

Paul had intended to stay there only while the persecution lasted. But by the time it was over, he had fallen in love with the life of prayer. He felt so close to God. How could he give that up? He decided to stay in the desert and never return to his wealthy city life. Instead, he would spend his life praying daily for the needs of all people and performing penance for sin.

There was another holy hermit at the same time named Anthony. Anthony thought he was the only hermit. God showed Paul to him in a dream and told Anthony to go visit him.

Paul was so happy to see Anthony because he knew he was going to die in a few days. Anthony was sad because he did not want to lose his new friend so soon. But, as Paul predicted, he died on January 15, 342. Anthony buried him in a cloak that had belonged to St. Athanasius. Then Anthony took home and treasured the garment of palm leaves that Paul had been wearing. He never forgot his wonderful friend.

We can treasure a keepsake, even a beautiful memory, of someone we love who has died. This way we feel them close to us until we meet them again in heaven.

JANUARY 16

ST. BERARD AND COMPANIONS

Six Franciscan friars accepted from St. Francis of Assisi an assignment to go to Morocco. They were to announce Christianity to the Muslims. Friars Berard, Peter, Adjutus, Accursio and Odo traveled by ship in 1219. Morocco is in the northwest corner of Africa and the journey was long and dangerous. The group arrived at Seville, Spain. They started preaching immediately, on streets and in public squares. People treated them as if they were crazy and had them arrested. To save themselves from being sent back home, the friars declared they wanted to see the sultan. So the governor of Seville sent them to Morocco.

The sultan received the friars and gave them freedom to preach in the city. But some of the people did not like this. They complained to the authorities. The sultan tried to save the friars by sending them to live in Marrakech, on the west coast of Morocco. A Christian prince and friend of the sultan, Dom Pedro Fernandez, took them into his home. But the friars knew that their mission was to preach the faith. They returned to the city as often as they could. This angered some people who did not want to hear the friars' message. These complaints angered the sultan so much that one day when he saw the friars preaching, he ordered them to stop or leave the country. Since they did not feel justified about doing either one, they were beheaded right then and there. It was January 16, 1220.

Dom Pedro went to claim the bodies of the martyrs. Eventually he brought their relics to Holy Cross Church in Coimbra, Portugal. The friars' mission to Morocco had been brief and an apparent failure. But the results were surprising. The story of these heroes fired the first Franciscans with the desire to be missionaries and martyrs too. It was their particular witness that inspired a young man to dedicate his life to God as a Franciscan priest. We know him as St. Anthony of Padua. His feast day is June 13.

As long as we try our best, we don't have to worry about the success or failure of what we do. God can use our effort and dedication to help people live better lives.

❦

JANUARY 17

ST. ANTHONY OF EGYPT

St. Anthony was born in 251 in a small village in Egypt. When he was twenty years old, his parents died. They left him a large estate and placed him in charge of the care of his young sister. Anthony felt overwhelmed and turned to God in prayer. Gradually he became more and more aware of the power of God in his life. About six months later, he heard this quotation of Jesus from the Gospel: "Go, sell what you own and give the money to the poor, and you will have treasure in heaven" (Mark 10:21). He took the words as a personal message in answer to his prayer for guidance. He sold most of his possessions keeping only enough to support his sister and himself. Then he gave the rest of the money to people who needed it.

Anthony's sister joined a group of women living a life of prayer and contemplation. Anthony decided to become a hermit. He begged an elderly hermit to teach him the spiritual life. Anthony also visited other hermits so he could learn each one's most outstanding virtue. Then he began his own life of prayer and penance alone with God.

When he was fifty-five, Anthony built a monastery to help others. Many people heard of him and sought his advice. He would give them practical advice such as: "The devil is afraid of us when we pray and make sacrifices. He is also afraid when we are humble and good. He is especially afraid when we love Jesus very much. He runs away when we make the Sign of the Cross."

St. Anthony visited Paul the hermit whose feast is celebrated on January 15. He felt enriched by the example of Paul's holy life. Anthony died after a long, prayerful life. He was 105. St. Athanasius wrote a well-known biography of St. Anthony of Egypt. St. Athanasius' feast day is May 2.

We should never become discouraged when the devil tempts us to do wrong. Remember that Jesus is right beside us. If we pray, he will help us. He will reward us for our love and faithfulness.

BLESSED CHRISTINA

Blessed Christina lived in the sixteenth century. She was born in Abruzzi, Italy. Her baptismal name was Matthia. As she grew up, Matthia felt the call to a life of prayer and penance. She chose to become a cloistered nun. Matthia entered the convent of St. Augustine in Aquila. She was called Sister Christina.

Sister Christina's life as a nun was hidden and silent. But the people of Aquila began to find out about the beauty of her vocation. She and the other nuns were bringing many blessings to them through their prayerful dedication. Sister Christina was cloistered but she was very aware of the needs of the poor people of her area. She and the nuns provided for them whatever they could. Sister Christina also kept herself aware of the crosses and sufferings people experienced. She prayed and offered penances to the Lord for their intentions.

Jesus blessed Sister Christina with ecstasies and the ability on occasion to know the future. The Lord even used her to work miracles for the good of others. When she died, the little children of Aquila went through the streets shouting that the holy nun was dead. It was January 18, 1543. A large crowd of people came to honor and thank her for the gift she had been for their city.

We can ask Blessed Christina to help us appreciate the importance of prayer in our everyday life.

JANUARY 19

ST. CANUTE

St. Canute was a strong, wise king of Denmark. He lived in the eleventh century. Canute was a great athlete, an expert horseman, and a marvelous general.

At the beginning of his reign, he led a war against the barbarians who were threatening to take over the civilized world. King Canute and his army defeated them. He loved the Christian faith so much that he introduced it to people who had never heard of Christianity.

St. Canute knelt in church at the foot of the altar and offered his crown to the King of kings, Jesus. King Canute was very charitable and gentle with his people. He tried to help them with their problems. Most of all, he wanted to help them be true followers of Jesus.

However, a rebellion broke out in his kingdom because of the laws he had made about supporting the Church. One day some angry people went to the church where Canute was praying. He knew they had come to harm him. While his enemies were still outside, King Canute received the sacraments of Reconciliation and Holy Communion. He felt compassion for those who were upset enough to kill him. With all his heart he forgave his enemies. Then, as he prayed, a spear was thrown through a window and he was killed. It was July 10, 1086.

St. Canute tried to be a good king so he could thank Jesus for all the blessings he had received. We, too, should thank God every day and offer him a crown made up of good deeds.

❧

JANUARY 20

ST. FABIAN AND ST. SEBASTIAN

Fabian was a pope who died a martyr in 250. It was during the persecution by Emperor Decius. Early writers say that 'he was an extraordinary person, known to be very holy. In a letter written shortly after Fabian's death, St. Cyprian explained how Fabian had been elected pope. The group who had gathered to elect the next pope received a real sign that the choice should be Fabian. He was the first layman to be pope. Bishop and martyr, Fabian's remains are now in the basilica of St. Sebastian. And the two martyrs share the same feast day.

Sebastian became widely known from the early centuries of the Church. As a Roman captain, he became known for his goodness and bravery. During the persecution by Diocletian, Sebastian would not renounce his Christian faith. Archers shot arrows into his body and left him for dead. When a holy widow came to bury him, she was shocked to find him still alive. She took him to her home and nursed his wounds. When Sebastian was well enough, the widow tried to persuade him to escape the dangers of Rome. But Sebastian was a brave soldier. He would not run away. He even approached Diocletian and urged him to stop persecuting the Christians.

The emperor was shocked to see Sebastian alive. He refused to listen to what the soldier had to say. Diocletian ordered that Sebastian be immediately clubbed to death. He died in 288.

Fabian was a pope and Sebastian was a soldier. They teach us that Jesus loves us individually and as we are. Like Fabian and Sebastian, we, too, have a gift to give. Our gift might be to fulfill a role of great responsibility like Fabian or to be a dedicated soldier like Sebastian. The important thing is to give our gift totally, like they did.

❧

JANUARY 21

ST. AGNES

St. Agnes was a Roman girl who died in 304. She was just twelve years old when she suffered martyrdom for her faith. Although few historical details remain, St. Agnes has always been popular. This is especially because St. Ambrose and other

well-known early Church saints have written about her. Agnes loved Jesus so much that she chose only him for her husband. Since she was beautiful, many young men wished to marry her. However, Agnes wanted to give her heart only to Jesus. She would always say, "Jesus is my only husband." She even turned down the governor's son, who became very angry. He tried to win her for his wife with gifts and promises. Agnes just kept telling him, "I am already promised to the Lord."

Agnes was accused of being a Christian and brought to the governor. The governor promised Agnes wonderful gifts if she would only deny God, but the girl refused. The governor tried to scare her by putting her in chains, but even then she did not back down. Agnes suffered other tortures. Finally, she was condemned and killed.

Agnes is buried in a cemetery named after her. In 354, Emperor Constantine's daughter built a large church there and had Agnes' body placed under the altar.

Agnes made heroic decisions and stuck to them. She could do this because she centered her young life in Jesus. She asked the Lord for the strength to be true to her Christian commitment. Her love for Jesus gave her the strength she needed. We can ask St. Agnes for her courage and love for Jesus.

ST. VINCENT OF SARAGOSSA

Vincent was martyred in Spain in 304. This was the same year that Agnes was martyred in Rome. They both were victims of the cruel persecution of Emperor Dacian.

Vincent had grown up in Saragossa, Spain. He was educated by the bishop, St. Valerius. The bishop had made Vincent a deacon. Even though Vincent was quite young, Valerius recognized his talents and goodness. Bishop Valerius asked him to preach and teach about Jesus and the Church.

Emperor Dacian arrested both Valerius and Vincent. He kept them in jail for a long time. They would not let themselves become downhearted. Both remained faithful to Jesus. Then the emperor sent Bishop Valerius into exile, but he sent Deacon Vincent to be cruelly tortured.

Vincent asked the Holy Spirit for strength. He wanted to be true to Jesus no matter how terrible things would be for him. The Lord granted him that strength. Deacon Vincent remained peaceful through all his sufferings. When the torture sessions were over, he was returned to prison where he converted the jailer. Finally, the emperor gave in and permitted people to visit Vincent. The Christians came and cared for his wounds. They tried their best to make him comfortable. It was not long before he died.

Vincent remained strong during persecution because of the influence of the holy bishop, Valerius. Vincent had learned from the bishop what it takes to be a follower of Jesus. St. Vincent will help us recognize and follow the good example of people if we ask him.

❦

JANUARY 23

ST. JOHN THE ALMSGIVER

John was a dedicated Christian nobleman. He used his wealth and position to help poor people. After his wife passed away, John became a priest and bishop. In 608, he was consecrated the patriarch of Alexandria, Egypt. What could people expect of this man who now had such an important position? St. John went to his new ministry focused on healing the divisions among his people. He pledged himself to practice a "charity without limits." The first thing he did was ask for a complete list of his "masters." He was asked to explain. He meant the poor. When they were counted, the poor of Alexandria numbered 7,500. St. John pledged to be their personal protector.

As patriarch, St. John proclaimed laws and issued reforms. He was respectful and kind, but firm. He devoted two days each week, Wednesday and Friday, to making himself available for anyone who wished to see him. People lined up and waited patiently for their turn. Some were rich.

Some were homeless and destitute. All received the same respect and attention. When he found out that the church treasury had eighty thousand pieces of gold, he divided it all among the hospitals and monasteries. He set up a system so that poor people received adequate money and means to support themselves. Refugees from neighboring areas were welcomed warmly. After the Persians had plundered Jerusalem, St. John sent money and supplies to the suffering people. He even sent Egyptian workmen to assist in rebuilding the churches there.

When people wanted to know how St. John could be so charitable and unselfish, he had an amazing answer. Once when he was very young he had a dream or vision. He saw a beautiful girl and he realized that she represented "charity." She told him: "I am the oldest daughter of the King. If you are devoted to me, I will lead you to Jesus. No one is as powerful with him as I am. Remember, it was for me that he became a baby to redeem humankind." St. John never tired of telling about that vision. He gently led the rich to be generous. He helped the poor trust that God would always be there for them.

St. John died peacefully on November 11, 619. Because of his great charity, he is called "the almsgiver."

Sometimes we might be tempted to just take care of "number one." When we have thoughts and attitudes like this, we can pray to St. John the Almsgiver. We can ask him for a share of his generous heart.

JANUARY 24

ST. FRANCIS DE SALES

Francis was born at the de Sales castle in Savoy, France, on August 21, 1567. His wealthy family provided him with an excellent education. By the age of twenty-four, Francis was a Doctor of Law. He returned to Savoy and led a hard-working life. He did not seem interested in important positions or a social life. In his heart, Francis was listening to a call that kept coming back like an echo. It seemed to be an invitation from the Lord to become a priest. Francis finally tried to explain his struggle to his family. His father was very disappointed. He wanted Francis to be a great man of the world. Family influence could have accomplished that goal. Instead, Francis became a priest on December 18, 1593.

Father de Sales lived in times when Christians were bitterly divided. He volunteered to go to a dangerous area of France to win back Catholics who had become Protestants. His father protested. He said it was bad enough that he had permitted Francis to become a priest. He was not going to let him be a martyr as well. But Francis believed that the Lord would protect him. He and his cousin, Father Louis de Sales, set out on foot for the Duchy of Chablais. The two priests soon learned how to live with insults and physical discomforts. Their lives were frequently in danger. Little by little, however, people returned to the Church.

The Conversion of The Sword of the Spirit

Francis eventually became the bishop of Geneva, Switzerland. With the help of St. Jane de Chantal, he started a religious order of sisters in 1610. These women are called the order of the Visitation. Francis wrote wonderful books about the spiritual life and the way to become holy. The books, *Treatise on the Love of God* and *Introduction to the Devout Life*, are still in print today. They are considered spiritual "classics."

Bishop de Sales died on December 28, 1622, at the age of fifty-six. He was declared a saint by Pope Innocent X in 1665. Because of his heroic dedication to the Church, he was given the special title "Doctor of the Church." He is also the patron saint of journalists.

We can learn many lessons from this great saint. He shows us that we can accomplish much good in our lifetime. We can ask St. Francis de Sales to help us listen to the Lord's voice and trust in his help.

~

JANUARY 25

CONVERSION OF ST. PAUL

Paul lived at the time of Jesus but as far as we know they never met. Paul was first called Saul. As a young man, he was a very bright student of the Hebrew religion. When he grew older, he persecuted the followers of Jesus.

In the Bible's Acts of the Apostles, we read

about Saul's amazing conversion (chapters 9, 22, 26). What happened? One day, Paul was on his way to the city of Damascus to hunt down more Christians. Suddenly, a great light shone all around him. As he fell to the ground blind, he heard a voice say, "Saul, Saul, why are you persecuting me?" Saul answered, "Who are you, Sir?" And the voice said, "I am Jesus, the one you are persecuting." Saul was shocked and confused. After a few seconds, he asked, "What do you want me to do?" Jesus told him to continue on to Damascus and there he would be told what to do.

At that moment, through the power of God, Saul received the gift to believe in Jesus. Weak and trembling, he reached out for help. His companions led him into Damascus. The light had blinded him temporarily. Now that he was blind he could really "see" the truth. And Jesus had come personally to meet him, to invite him to conversion. Saul became a great lover of Jesus. After his baptism, he thought only of helping everyone know and love Jesus, the Savior.

We know Saul by his Roman name of Paul. He is called "the apostle." He traveled all over the world, preaching the Good News. He led countless people to Jesus. He worked and suffered. His enemies tried to kill him several times. Yet nothing could stop him. When he was old and tired, he was once again put in prison and sentenced to die. Still St. Paul was happy to suffer and even die for Christ.

This great apostle wrote marvelous letters to the Christians. They are in the Bible. These letters, called epistles, are read frequently during the Liturgy of the Word at Mass.

St. Paul's conversion was very important for the life of the Church. We are reminded that the Lord looks for us, too. He finds us along our Damascus road. He invites us to give up the things in our lives that keep him away. Will we recognize him as Paul did? Will we be willing to become real followers of Jesus as Paul was? Let us ask St. Paul to help us.

JANUARY 26

ST. TIMOTHY AND ST. TITUS

Besides being saints and bishops in the early Church, these two men have something else in common. Both received the gift of faith through the preaching of St. Paul.

Timothy was born in Lycaonia in Asia Minor. His mother was a Jew and his father was a Gentile. When Paul came to preach in Lycaonia, Timothy, his mother and his grandmother all became Christians. Several years later, Paul went back and found Timothy grown up. He felt that Timothy had a call from God to be a missionary. Paul invited him to join him in preaching the Gospel. So it was that Timothy left his home and parents to follow Paul. He was soon to share in Paul's sufferings as well. They would have the joy of bringing the Word of God to many people. Timothy was the great apostle's beloved disciple, like a son to him. He went everywhere with Paul until he became bishop of Ephesus. Then Timothy stayed there to shepherd his people. As St. Paul, Timothy, too, died a martyr.

Titus was a Gentile nonbeliever. He, too, became Paul's disciple. Titus was generous and hard-working. He joyfully preached the Good News with Paul on their missionary travels. Because Titus was so trustworthy, Paul freely sent him on many "missions" to the Christian communities. Titus helped people strengthen their faith in Jesus. He was able to restore peace when there were arguments among the Christians. Titus had a special gift for being a peacemaker. Paul appreciated this gift in Titus and recognized it as the Holy Spirit's work. Paul would send Titus to iron out difficulties. When Titus would arrive among a group of Christians, the guilty ones would feel sorry. They would ask forgiveness and would make up for what they had done. When peace was restored, Titus would go back and tell Paul about the good results. This brought Paul and the first Christians much happiness.

St. Paul made Titus bishop of the island of Crete, where he stayed until his death.

Timothy and Titus gave their whole life—their time and energy—to Jesus. They were true disciples of St. Paul. It's easy to overlook people like this or take them for granted. Let's say some prayers today for all who spread the Good News as Paul, Timothy and Titus did.

JANUARY 27

ST. ANGELA MERICI

Angela was born in the small Italian town of Desenzano, Italy, around 1474. Her parents died when she was ten. She and her only sister, who was three years older, loved each other very much. A wealthy uncle took the girls into his home. Still suffering from the loss of her parents, Angela was struck again when her sister also passed away. The older girl had died even before a priest could arrive to administer the last sacraments. Angela worried about her sister's soul. Jesus revealed to her that the girl had been saved. Angela felt peace return to her own soul. She thanked the Lord in prayer. She wanted to do something to show her gratitude. This desire led her to promise to spend the rest of her life serving Jesus totally.

When she was about twenty-two, Angela began to notice that the children of her town knew little about their religion. Angela invited some of her girlfriends to join her in teaching religion classes. Angela's friends were anxious to help her with the children.

At that time there were no religious orders of teaching sisters. No one had ever thought of such a thing. St. Angela Merici was the first to gather together a group of women to open schools for children. On November 25, 1535, twenty-eight young women offered their lives to God. It was the beginning of the Ursuline order. Angela placed the congregation under the protection of St. Ursula. This is how they got their name. The women remained in their own homes at first. Because of many difficulties, it was a long time before they could live together in a convent. Angela died on January 27, 1540, when her congregation was still in its beginning stages. Her trust in God had gotten her through many hard tests in her lifetime. There was no doubt in her mind that the Lord would take care of the mission she had begun. And so he did.

The Ursuline Sisters have spread to many countries. The order continues its works for Jesus and his Church, especially in the education of children and young adults. Angela was proclaimed a saint by Pope Pius VI in 1807.

Angela Merici reminds us that our own struggles and disappointments can help us see the hurts of others. When we are willing to reach out, the Lord will use us to do his wonderful work. Let us ask St. Angela to show us how to be sensitive and compassionate.

JANUARY 28

ST. THOMAS AQUINAS

Thomas lived in the thirteenth century. He was the son of a noble family of Italy. He was very intelligent, but he never boasted about it. He knew that his mind was a gift from God. Thomas was one of nine children. His parents hoped that he would become a Benedictine abbot some day. The family castle was in Rocca Secca, just north of Monte Cassino where the monks lived.

Thomas was sent to the abbey for schooling when he was five. When he was eighteen, he went to Naples to finish his studies. There he met a new group of religious men called the Order of Preachers. Their founder, St. Dominic, was still living. Thomas knew he wanted to become a priest. He felt that he was called to join these men who would become known in popular language as "Dominicans." His parents were angry with him. When he was on his way to Paris to study, his brothers kidnapped him. They kept him a prisoner in one of their castles for over a year. During that time, they did all they could to make him change his mind. One of his sisters, too, came to persuade him to give up his vocation. But Thomas spoke so beautifully about the joy of serving God that she changed her mind. She decided to give her life to God as a nun. After fifteen months, Thomas was finally freed to follow his call.

St. Thomas wrote so well about God that people all over the world have used his books for hundreds of years. His explanations about God and the faith came from Thomas' great love for God. He was effective because he wasn't trying to make an impression on anyone. He just wanted with all his heart to offer the gift of his life to Jesus and the Church. St. Thomas is one of the greatest Doctors of the Church.

Around the end of 1273, Pope Gregory X asked Thomas to be part of an important Church meeting called the Council of Lyons. While traveling to the meeting, Thomas became ill. He had to stop at a monastery at Fossanova, Italy, where he died. It was March 7, 1274. He was only forty-nine. St. Thomas was declared a saint in 1323 by Pope Benedict XI.

All of St. Thomas' learning, writing or teaching is not what makes him a saint. He became a saint by doing everything for God with love. He will help us do the same if we ask him.

ST. GILDAS

This saint was born around the year 500 in Britain. He set out as a young man to practice a self-sacrificing lifestyle. He did this to help himself become closer to God. Gildas was serious about his Christian commitment. He felt the responsibility to pray and sacrifice for the sins committed by the people of his times. He wrote sermons trying to convince people to give up wickedness. He encouraged them to stop their lives of scandal. Because Gildas cared so much, his writings sometimes seemed overly critical. Actually, he didn't mean to condemn anyone. He was begging people to turn to God.

Gildas was a spiritual man who lived a hermit's life. He didn't choose a quiet, prayerful life because he wanted to keep away from the world around him. He chose his life to help him grow closer to God. He was more aware than the average person of some things that were very wrong in society. Sadly, many people were not aware enough of God and his law. They did not even realize the evils that were destroying them. That is why some people in the Church—priests, bishops and laymen and women—went to Gildas for advice about deeply spiritual matters.

Toward the end of his life, Gildas lived his hermit's life on a tiny island in Brittany. Even though he wanted to be alone to prepare his soul for death, disciples followed him there. He welcomed them as a sign that the Lord wanted him to share his spiritual gifts with others.

Gildas was like the "conscience" of society. Sometimes we don't like to hear about sin, but sin is real. Sometimes we, too, are tempted to do wrong or are neglectful. Then we can say a little prayer to St. Gildas. We can ask him to obtain for us the will power to do the right thing.

JANUARY 30

ST. BATHILDIS

The story begins around the year 630. A frightened, Christian English girl could have never imagined what her future would be like. What she did know was that she had been kidnapped and was on a pirate ship. Where was she going? Who could she ask? Finally, the ship docked and she heard people saying they were in France. Bathildis was quickly sold as a slave to the manager of King Clovis' palace.

The rest of the story is like a Cinderella fairy tale, except that this tale is really true. The quiet girl paid careful attention as her chores were explained or demonstrated to her. Day after day, she went from one task to another doing the very best she could. She was shy and gentle, but even King Clovis began to notice her. The more he observed, the more he was impressed. This was the kind of girl who would make a wonderful wife—even a king's wife. In 649, Clovis married Bathildis. The little slave girl had become the queen. They had three sons. Clovis died when the oldest son was only five, so Bathildis would be ruler of France until her sons grew up.

It must have been surprising to just about everybody that Bathildis could rule so wisely. She remembered too well what it was like to be poor. She remembered also her years as a slave. She had been sold as if she were a "thing of little value." Bathildis wanted everyone to know how precious they were to God. She was filled with love for Jesus and his Church. She used her position to help the Church in every way she could. She did not become proud or arrogant. Rather, she cared for the poor. She also protected people from being captured and treated as slaves. She filled France with hospitals. She started a seminary to train priests and a convent for nuns. Later, Queen Bathildis entered the convent herself. As a nun, she set aside her royal dignity. She became one of the nuns, humble and obedient. She never demanded or even expected that other people should wait on her. She was also very kind and gentle with the sick. When she became ill, she suffered a long, painful illness until her death on January 30, 680.

Queen Bathildis' life shows us how each day is a new beginning. It can bring wonderful surprises. So when we are afraid because we do not know what is happening, we can ask St. Bathildis to show us how to trust God.

ST. JOHN BOSCO

John Bosco was born in Turin, Italy, on August 16, 1815. His parents were poor farmers. When John was two, his father died. John's mother struggled to keep the family together. As soon as he was old enough, John, too, worked as hard as he could to help his mother. He was intelligent and full of life. John started to think about becoming a priest. He didn't say anything to his mother because he knew they couldn't afford the seminary education. Besides, his mother needed help at home. So John waited and prayed and hoped. Finally, a holy priest, St. Joseph Cafasso, became aware of John's desire to be a priest. Father Cafasso helped him enter the seminary. John had to work his way through school. He learned to do all kinds of trades. He was a carpenter, a shoemaker, a cook, a pastry maker and a farmer. He did many other jobs as well. He could never have guessed how much this practical experience would help others later. John became a priest in 1841. As a priest, Don Bosco, which means Father Bosco, began his great ministry. He gathered together homeless boys and taught them trades. This way they would not have to steal or get into trouble. By 1850, there were 150 boys living at his home for boys. Don Bosco's mother was the housekeeper. At first, people did not understand what

Don Bosco was trying to do. They were afraid that the boys would never really turn out well. But Don Bosco proved that they would.

"Do you want to be Don Bosco's friend?" he would ask each new boy who came to him. "You do?" he would ask happily. "Then, you must help me save your soul," he would conclude. Every night he wanted his boys to say three Hail Mary's, so that the Blessed Mother would help them keep away from sin. He also recommended that they receive the sacraments of Reconciliation and Holy Communion often and with love. One of Don Bosco's boys became a saint, St. Dominic Savio.

Don Bosco started his own religious order of priests and brothers. They were called the Salesians, after St. Francis de Sales. An order of Salesian sisters was started, too, with the help of St. Mary Mazzarello. Don Bosco died on January 31, 1888. The entire city of Turin lined the streets to pay him tribute. His funeral became a joyous proclamation of thanksgiving to God for the life of this wonderful man. A young parish priest who had once met Don Bosco later became Pope Pius XI. He had the joy of declaring Don Bosco a saint in 1934.

We can learn from Don Bosco what an impact for good one person can make. Isn't it a wonderful thing to reach out cheerfully to help others?

fEBRuARy

FEBRUARY 1

ST. BRIGID OF IRELAND

A few years after St. Patrick arrived in Ireland, a little girl named Brigid was born. Her father was an Irish lord named Dubthac and her mother was named Brocca.

As Brigid grew up, she deepened her love for Jesus. She looked for him in the poor and often brought food and clothing to them. It has been said that one day she gave away a whole pail of milk. Then she began to worry about what her mother would say. She prayed to the Lord to make up for what she had given away. When she got home, her pail was full again.

Brigid was very pretty. Her father thought that it was time for her to marry. However, she had decided in her heart to give herself entirely to God. She did not want to marry anyone. When she learned that her beauty was the reason young men were attracted to her, she made an unusual request to God. She asked that her beauty be taken from her. God granted her request. Seeing that his daughter was no longer pretty, Brigid's father gladly agreed when Brigid asked to become a nun.

The girl did follow her call to religious life. She even started a convent so that other young women could become nuns, too. It seems that after she consecrated her life to God in the convent, a miracle happened. Brigid became beautiful again! She reminded people of the Blessed Mother because she was so lovely and gentle. Some called her the "Mary of the Irish." St. Brigid died in 525.

Jesus loves each one of us. We look the way he wants us to. Brigid concentrated on important values such as the meaning of her life and helping less fortunate people. She reminds us not to waste our time worrying about whether we are nice looking or plain. Each of us is special to God.

❦

FEBRUARY 2

PRESENTATION OF THE LORD

Forty days after Jesus was born, Mary and Joseph brought the Child to the great Temple in Jerusalem. There they presented Jesus to the Heavenly Father. That was the Jewish law. The Holy Family obeyed it with loving hearts.

While they were in the Temple, Mary also fulfilled another requirement of the law. After the birth of their children, all Jewish mothers were supposed to go to the Temple for the ceremony called the Purification. Mary did her duty cheerfully. She teaches us to be humble and obedient as she was.

A holy old priest of the Temple named Simeon learned from God that the Infant Jesus was truly the Savior. With what joy he held Mary's Son in his arms. "My own eyes are looking at my salvation," he exclaimed. God let him recognize Jesus as the Savior and Simeon put his trust in the little Child. Imagine what Mary and Joseph were thinking. Then, inspired by God, Simeon told Mary that she would have to suffer very much. He was talking about the terrible pain our Blessed Mother would feel when Jesus died on the cross.

This feast of the Presentation reminds us that we belong to God first of all. Because he is our Father and Creator, we owe him our loving obedience.

We, too, can imitate Mary and Joseph. We can cheerfully obey our parents, guardians and teachers in all that is right. We can ask the Holy Family to help us live responsibly every day of our lives.

☙

FEBRUARY 3

ST. BLASE

St. Blase lived in the fourth century. Some say that he came from a rich family and received a Christian education. As a young man, Blase thought about all the sufferings and troubles of the times. He began to realize that only spiritual joys can make a person really happy. He became a priest and then bishop of Sebaste in Armenia which is now modern Turkey. With all his heart, Blase worked to make his people holy and happy. He prayed and preached; he tried to help everyone.

When the governor, Licinius, began to perse-cute the Christians, St. Blase was captured. He was sent to prison to be beheaded. On the way, people crowded the road to see their beloved bishop for the last time. He blessed them all, even the pagans. A poor mother rushed up to him. She begged him to save her child who was choking to death from a fishbone. The saint whispered a prayer and blessed the child. He worked a miracle that saved the child's life. That is why St. Blase is called upon by all who have throat diseases. On his feast day, we have our throats blessed. We ask him to protect us from all sicknesses of the throat.

In prison, the saintly bishop converted many pagans. No torture could make him give up his faith in Jesus. He was beheaded in the year 316. Now St. Blase is with Jesus forever.

Today let us honor St. Blase by going without that candy bar or ice cream cone we planned to have.

❧

FEBRUARY 4

ST. JANE VALOIS

St. Jane was the daughter of King Louis XI of France. She was born in 1464. Since the king wanted a son, he was very disappointed when Jane was born. He did not even want his little daughter to live at the palace because she was deformed. When the princess was just five years old, she was sent to live with other people. Despite the way she was treated by her own father, Jane was good and gentle with everyone. She was convinced that Jesus and Mary loved her. Jane also believed that the Lord would use her to do good in his name. And she was right.

When she grew up, Jane decided that she did not want to marry. She had given herself to Jesus and his Blessed Mother. But her father ignored her personal choice. He forced her to marry the duke of Orleans. Jane was a devoted wife for twenty-two years. After the duke became king, however, he sent Jane to live by herself in a far-off township. The queen did not let herself become resentful. Instead, she exclaimed: "God be praised! He has permitted this that I may serve him better than I have up until now."

Jane lived a prayerful life. She practiced penances and acts of kindness. She gave all her money to the poor. She even started an order of sisters called the Sisters of the Annunciation of the Blessed Virgin Mary. She spent the rest of her life joyfully for Jesus and his Mother. St. Jane died in 1505. She was proclaimed a saint by Pope Pius XII in 1950.

When we find someone or some situation hurtful, let us remember St. Jane Valois. We can ask her to help us be as patient and forgiving as she was.

FEBRUARY 5

ST. AGATHA

A beautiful Christian girl named Agatha lived in Sicily in the third century. The governor heard of Agatha's beauty and brought her to his palace. He wanted to make her commit sins against purity, but she was brave and would not give in. "My Lord Jesus Christ," she prayed, "you see my heart and you know my desire. You alone must have me, because I am all yours. Save me from this evil man. Make me worthy of winning out over the devil."

The governor tried sending Agatha to the house of a wicked woman. Perhaps the girl would change for the worse. But Agatha had great trust in God and prayed all the time. She kept herself pure. She would not listen to the evil suggestions of the woman and her daughters. After a month, she was brought back to the governor. He tried again to win her. "You are a noblewoman," he said kindly. "Why have you lowered yourself to be a humble Christian?"

"Even though I am a noble," answered Agatha, "I am a slave of Jesus Christ."

"Then what does it really mean to be noble?" the governor asked.

Agatha answered, "It means to serve God."

When he realized that she would not sin, the governor became angry. He had Agatha whipped and tortured. As she was being carried back to

prison she whispered, "Lord, my Creator, you have protected me from the cradle. You have taken me from the love of the world and given me patience to suffer. Now receive my soul."

Agatha died a martyr at Catania, Sicily, in the year 250.

Let us learn from St. Agatha's example. Like her, we can pray with all our heart when we are tempted to do anything wrong.

❦

FEBRUARY 6

ST. PAUL MIKI AND COMPANIONS

These twenty-six martyrs are sometimes called the martyrs of Nagasaki and the martyrs of Japan. St. Francis Xavier brought the Good News of Christianity to Japan in 1549. Many received the Word and were baptized by St. Francis himself. Although Francis moved on and eventually died near the shores of China, the faith had grown in Japan. By 1587 there were over two hundred thousand Catholics. Missionaries from various religious orders were there. Japanese priests, religious and lay people lived the faith joyfully.

In 1597, forty-five years after the arrival of Francis Xavier, a powerful Japanese official, Hideyoshi, listened to the gossip of a Spanish merchant. The merchant whispered that the missionaries were traitors of Japan. He suggested that these traitors would cause Japan to be defeated by Spain and Portugal. The claim was false and absurd. But as an overreaction, Hideyoshi had twenty-six people arrested. The group included six Franciscans from Spain, Mexico and India; three Japanese Jesuit catechists, including St. Paul Miki; and seventeen Japanese Catholic lay people, including children.

The twenty-six were led to the place of execution outside Nagasaki. They were fastened to individual crosses with chains and cords and had iron collars clamped around their necks. Each cross was hoisted and the base was lowered into a hole dug for it. Spears were thrust into each of the victims. They died almost at the same moment. Their blood-stained clothes were treasured by the Christian community and miracles happened through their intercession.

Each martyr was a gift to the Church. St. Paul Miki, a Jesuit catechist, had been a great preacher. His last valiant homily came from the cross as he encouraged the Christian community to be faithful until death. It was February 5, 1597. St. Paul Miki and his companions were proclaimed saints by Pope Gregory XVI in 1862.

We can pray every day for people who live in parts of the world where they are persecuted for their beliefs. We can also ask St. Paul Miki and his companions for courage to be faithful to Jesus.

FEBRUARY 7

BLESSED GILES MARY

His complete name as a religious was Brother Giles Mary-of-St.-Joseph. Brother Giles Mary was born near Taranto, Italy, in 1729. As a child he learned rope-making and was good at his trade.

When he was twenty-five, Giles became aware of a call from the Lord to enter a religious order and give his life to God. Giles entered the Friars of St. Peter Alcantara in Naples. And what extraordinary things did he do to be proclaimed "blessed"? He was singled out for such an honor because of two virtues that guided his whole religious life. The virtues were simplicity and humility.

Brother Giles Mary tried to approach each day with an attitude of wanting to serve God. He was grateful for his calling and it showed. Brother Giles walked up and down the halls where he lived. He was the porter. He opened the door promptly and with a smile every time a visitor pulled the rope that rang the bell. He took gentle care of the poor, the homeless, the ill who came to that door. He was given the responsibility of distributing the food and alms that his community could spare. Brother Giles Mary loved to do that. No matter how much he gave to needy people, so much remained for others. He knew it was St. Joseph who did this. After all, St. Joseph had once taken such good care of Jesus and Mary. Brother

Giles Mary spread devotion to St. Joseph through-out his whole religious life.

After a life of faithfulness to God and his cho-sen vocation, Brother Giles Mary-of-St.-Joseph died on February 7, 1812. He was declared "blessed" by Pope Pius IX in 1888.

We can learn from Blessed Giles' life. It won't be great things or important responsibilities that make us successful with God. What God looks for is a generous heart and faithfulness in what we do.

FEBRUARY 8

ST. JEROME EMILIANI

Jerome was born in 1486, the son of a noble family of Venice, Italy. He was a good soldier and was put in command of a fortress high in the mountains. While defending this post from an in-vasion by some troops of Maximilian I, he was taken prisoner and thrown into a dungeon. Chained in that miserable prison, he began to re-gret the careless way he had been living. He was sorry that he had thought so little about God. He was sorry for wasting several years in immoral living. Jerome promised the Blessed Mother that he would change his life if she would help him. His prayers were answered and he escaped to safety. It is said that Jerome, with a grateful heart, went straight to a church. He hung his prison chains in front of Mary's altar.

The young man eventually became a priest. He was devoted to works of charity. His special concern was for the many homeless orphan children he found in the streets. He rented a house for them, and gave them clothes and food. He instructed them in the truths of the faith.

St. Jerome started a religious congregation of men called the Company of the Servants of the Poor. They would care for the poor, especially orphans, and would teach youth. He did all he could for the peasants, too. He would work with them in the fields. St. Jerome would talk to them of God's goodness while he worked by their side. He died while caring for plague victims in 1537. He was proclaimed a saint by Pope Benedict XIV in 1767.

St. Jerome Emiliani was a gift to the people of his time and to all the Church. By totally turning his life around, he became an image of the love of God. He gave hope to those who were poor and abandoned. In 1928, Pope Pius XI named him the patron saint of orphans and homeless children.

We can ask St. Jerome Emiliani to help us see the importance of being a good example. We can ask him to help us recognize the opportunities we have to witness to our love for Jesus, Mary and our Catholic faith.

ST. APOLLONIA AND THE MARTYRS OF ALEXANDRIA

A holy virgin, Apollonia, lived in Alexandria, Egypt, in the third century. Christians were being persecuted there during the reign of Emperor Philip. Apollonia had spent her whole life serving God. Now that she was growing old, she was not about to take time to rest. She bravely risked her life to comfort suffering Christians in prison. "Remember that your trials will not last long," she would say. "But the joys of heaven will last forever."

It was just a matter of time until Apollonia, too, was captured. When the judge asked her name, she courageously said, "I am a Christian and I love and serve the true God."

Angry people tortured Apollonia, trying to force her to give up her faith. First, all her teeth were smashed and then knocked out. Strangely enough, that is why people frequently pray to St. Apollonia when they have a toothache. But even this painful ordeal did not shake the woman's faith. Apollonia was then told that if she did not deny Jesus, she would be thrown into a raging fire. The woman would not let her fear overcome her. She chose to die by fire rather than abandon her faith in Jesus. When the pagans saw how heroic she was, many were converted. Apollonia died around 249.

The martyrs greatly desired to shed their blood for Jesus. And what are we willing to do for him? Are we strong enough to stand a little inconvenience without pouting or complaining?

FEBRUARY 10

ST. SCHOLASTICA

Scholastica and St. Benedict were twins born in central Italy in 480. It is said that for many years, their parents had begged God to send them children. When at last Benedict and Scholastica were born, their parents cherished them. The couple tried to raise them well.

Scholastica was a friendly, intelligent girl. She promised herself to Jesus when she was still very young. After her parents died, she went to visit her brother who had already left home. He had built a big monastery and was the leader of many good monks. Benedict had become the founder of the Benedictine order.

St. Benedict was very good to his sister. When he realized that she and other young women wanted to become nuns, he helped them start a monastery for women. While Benedict was at Subiaco, Scholastica was at a nearby monastery.

When her twin brother moved to Monte Cassino, she entered a woman's monastery near there.

Once a year Benedict visited his sister and spent the day with her. On one of his visits, when he rose to leave, Scholastica begged him to stay longer. Benedict said he could not. His sister quietly bowed her head and begged the Lord to prolong her brother's visit. Suddenly, a storm arose and Benedict was unable to leave. He stayed and they talked all through the night. They spoke of the goodness of God and the happiness of the saints in heaven. Not long after, Scholastica passed away. She died in 547.

Scholastica and Benedict helped each other draw closer to God by the way they treated one other. We, too, can learn to value people who share with us their good example and spiritual attitudes.

❧

FEBRUARY 11

OUR LADY OF LOURDES

It was on February 11, 1858, that a beautiful lady first appeared to Bernadette Soubirous of Lourdes, France. Bernadette was a sickly girl. Her family was so poor they lived in a cellar that had once been a jail. Even though she was fourteen, Bernadette still could not read or write. She never could remember her catechism lessons, but she was a good girl. She loved God very much. Although her memory was poor, Bernadette kept trying hard to learn all she could about God. She was pure and obedient, too.

The beautiful lady Bernadette saw wore a white dress and a light blue sash. A white veil covered her head and fell over her shoulders to the ground. On her feet were two lovely golden roses. Her hands were joined and a rosary hung from her right arm. Its chain and cross shone like gold. The lovely lady encouraged Bernadette to say the Rosary. She appeared eighteen times to St. Bernadette. She asked her to tell the people to pray, to do penance and to recite the Rosary for sinners.

During the last apparition, Bernadette asked the beautiful lady who she was. The lady replied, "I am the Immaculate Conception." She was Mary, the Mother of God.

A large church called a basilica was built where Bernadette saw Our Lady. Although the apparitions took place over a hundred years ago, miracles still happen there. Many people are cured of sicknesses. Crippled people walk again. Blind people see again. Lonely, broken people find hope again. There, where she once appeared to St. Bernadette, Our Lady still shows her love for us.

Let us try to say the Rosary to our Blessed Mother every day. Through this prayer, we receive all the graces we need for ourselves and for those we love.

ST. MELETIUS

Meletius was called to shepherd the Church in the fourth century. The Roman persecutions were over and Constantine had recognized Christianity as a legal religion in 315. What, then, could have made Bishop Meletius' ministry so difficult? Storm clouds had gathered within the Church. Some considered themselves Catholic, some Arian. The Arian heresy denied that Jesus is divine. Some people believed the error because things were not so clear then.

Bishop Meletius loved the Church and was true to Jesus. He believed that Jesus is God and realized that the Church would have to speak up clearly about who Jesus is. Meletius became the bishop of Antioch in 361. The Arians were not pleased. For twenty years, Meletius was a patient, loving bishop. But his life was made difficult by people who did not accept him. He often had to go into hiding because other men were claiming to be the bishop of his diocese. But St. Meletius was the true bishop and would patiently return as soon as possible. When Emperor Valens died in 378, the Arians stopped their persecution.

In 381, the famous Council of Constantinople, a large Church meeting, was called. The bishops wanted to talk about important truths of our faith. Bishop Meletius opened the Church Council meetings and directed the sessions. Then, to the sadness of all the bishops, he died right there at one of the meetings.

Great saints like John Chrysostom and Gregory of Nyssa attended his funeral along with all the bishops at the Council. The people of Constantinople poured in to the church as well. St. Gregory of Nyssa delivered the funeral homily. He spoke of a meek, Christ-like bishop whom everyone loved. And he was right: everyone who loved the Church loved St. Meletius.

St. Gregory spoke of Bishop Meletius' calmness and radiant smile, his fatherly voice and gentle touch. St. Meletius died on February 12, 381.

Bishop Meletius was always kind and good-natured. Many people made his life difficult but he never lost his gentle ways. This is the real test of his goodness. This is how he proved his love for Jesus. We can do the same in little ways.

FEBRUARY 13

ST. CATHERINE OF RICCI

Alexandrina was born in 1522 into the Ricci family of Florence, Italy. At the age of thirteen, the girl entered the Dominican order. As a sister she chose the name Catherine.

Even at that young age, Catherine had a deep love for the passion of Jesus Christ. She used to think about Our Lord's sufferings often. Jesus gave her the great privilege of receiving in her own body the marks of his wounds. She was happy to accept all the pains of these wounds.

Catherine also felt very sorry for the poor souls suffering in purgatory. She realized how they longed to be with God in heaven. She realized, too, that this time in purgatory seemed to drag on endlessly. St. Catherine prayed and did penance for them. Once God let her know that a certain man was in purgatory. So great was her love that she offered to suffer for him. God listened to her prayer and she suffered greatly for forty days.

After a long, painful illness, St. Catherine died at the age of sixty-eight. It was February 2, 1590. She was proclaimed a saint by Pope Clement XII in 1747.

Let us help the poor souls in purgatory with our prayers as St. Catherine Ricci did. We pray that they soon may be with the Lord. When they are in heaven, they will pray for us.

FEBRUARY 14

ST. CYRIL AND ST. METHODIUS

These two brothers were from Thessalonica, Greece. Methodius was born in 815 and Cyril in 827. Both became priests and shared the same holy desires to spread the faith. They became missionaries to the Slav nations of Moravia, Bohemia and Bulgaria. This is how it happened: In 862, just seven years before Cyril's death, the prince of Moravia asked for missionaries. They would bring the Good News of Jesus and the Church to his country. The prince added one more request: that the missionaries speak the language of his people.

The two brothers, Cyril and Methodius, volunteered and were accepted. They realized that they were being asked to leave their own country, language and culture behind out of love for Jesus. They did this willingly. Cyril and Methodius invented a Slav alphabet. They translated the Bible and the Church's liturgy into the Slav language. Because of them, the people were able to receive Christianity in words they could understand.

Some in the Church at that time did not approve of the use of a native language in the Church's liturgy. The two brothers faced criticism. They were called to Rome to have a meeting with the pope. Some people may have been surprised at the way the meeting went. Pope Adrian II showed his gratitude and admiration for the two missionaries. He approved their methods of spreading the faith and named them bishops. It seems that Cyril, a monk, died before he could actually be consecrated a bishop but Methodius was. Cyril died on February 14, 869. He is buried in the Church of St. Clement in Rome. Methodius returned to the Slav countries and continued his labors for fifteen more years. He died on April 6, 885.

On December 31, 1980, Pope John Paul II declared St. Cyril and St. Methodius co-patrons of Europe along with St. Benedict.

Let us admire the generosity of these two holy brothers. We can ask them to inspire us with courage and kindness. They will help us be respectful of all people even if their religion, customs, language and culture may be different from our own.

❧

ST. FAUSTINUS AND ST. JOVITA

St. Faustinus and St. Jovita were brothers who lived in Brescia, Italy. They were among the early Christian martyrs. The two brothers suffered during the persecution of Emperor Hadrian in the second century.

From the time they were young, Faustinus and Jovita were well-known for their great love for their religion. They also performed works of Christian charity. They helped each other do good for the people who needed them. The bishop of Brescia made them both priests. They began to preach everywhere, to both the rich and the poor. They spared themselves no sacrifice to bring many people to God. Because it was a time of persecution, it was easy to be afraid. But Faustinus and Jovita would not give in to fear of the soldiers even though these soldiers were actually putting many Christians to death.

When the emperor heard that Faustinus and Jovita dared to preach openly, he sent them to prison and had them tortured. He hoped that torture would silence them. But no matter what the two priests suffered, they would not promise to stop preaching about Jesus. They kept an attitude of prayer even in that terrible prison. In fact, they willingly offered up their sufferings to the Lord. Faustinus and Jovita encouraged each other to be courageous even if they, too, would have to die as martyrs for Jesus.

Both brothers remained true to their belief in and love for Jesus until they were martyred. The exact date of their death was not recorded. Their heroic witness, however, is a sacred memory and challenge to all of us.

How pleased God is to see brothers and sisters helping one another to study and learn about their faith. Like St. Faustinus and St. Jovita, they can encourage each other to love and live for Jesus.

FEBRUARY 16

ST. ONESIMUS

Onesimus lived in the first century. He was a slave who robbed his master and ran away to Rome. In Rome he went to see the great apostle, St. Paul, who was a prisoner for his faith. Paul received Onesimus with the kindness and love of a good father. Paul helped the young man realize he had done wrong to steal. But more than that, he led Onesimus to believe in and accept the Christian faith.

After Onesimus became a Christian, Paul sent him back to his master, Philemon, who was Paul's friend. But Paul did not send the slave back alone and defenseless. He "armed" Onesimus with a brief, powerful letter. Paul hoped his letter would set everything right for his new friend, Onesimus. Paul wrote to Philemon: "I plead with you for my own son, for Onesimus. I am sending him back to you. Welcome him as though he were my very heart."

That touching letter is in the New Testament of the Bible. Philemon accepted Paul's letter and Paul's advice. When Onesimus returned to his master, he was set free. Later, he went back to St. Paul and became his faithful helper.

St. Paul made Onesimus a priest and then a bishop. The former slave dedicated the rest of his life to preaching the Good News that had changed his life forever. It is believed that during the persecutions, Onesimus was brought in chains to Rome and stoned to death.

If we should ever hurt anyone in any way, let us ask forgiveness right away. God will be pleased to see that we are sorry and he will bless us as he did Onesimus.

FEBRUARY 17

SEVEN FOUNDERS OF
THE SERVITE ORDER

These seven saints lived in the thirteenth century. They were all from Florence, Italy. Each had a great love for Mary, the Mother of God. They were active members of a confraternity of the Blessed Virgin Mary.

The way they came to be founders of the Servite order is remarkable. On the feast of the Assumption, while the seven men were deep in prayer, the Blessed Mother appeared to them. She inspired them to leave the world and to live alone with God. After several years of living as hermits, they went to their bishop. They asked him for a rule of life to follow. The bishop encouraged them to pray and to ask for guidance from Mary. Mary appeared to the men carrying a black habit. At her side was an angel bearing a scroll with the words "Servants of Mary" written on it. In this vision, the Blessed Mother said that she had chosen them to be her servants. She asked them to wear a black habit. This was the habit they started to wear in 1240. They also began to live their religious life according to the rule of St. Augustine.

These wonderful men helped each other love and serve God better. Six of them were ordained priests. They were Bonfilius, Amadeus, Hugh,

Sostenes, Manettus and Buonagiunta. The seventh founder, Alexis, remained a wonderful religious until death. In his humility, he chose not to be ordained to the priesthood.

Many young men came to join these holy founders. They were known as Servants of Mary or Servites.

The Servite order was approved by the Vatican in 1259. The seven holy founders were declared saints by Pope Leo XIII in 1888.

Like these seven saints, let us love our Blessed Mother and ask her to help us in every need.

FEBRUARY 18

ST. BERNADETTE

St. Bernadette was born in Lourdes, France, on January 7, 1844. Her parents were very poor. Bernadette was frail and often sick.

On Thursday, February 11, 1859, Bernadette was sent with her younger sister and a friend to gather firewood. A beautiful lady appeared to her above a rosebush in the grotto of Massabielle. The lady was dressed in blue and white. She smiled at Bernadette. Then she made the sign of the cross with a rosary of ivory and gold. Bernadette fell on her knees. She took out her own rosary and began to say it.

The beautiful lady was God's Mother, the Blessed Virgin Mary. She appeared to Bernadette seventeen times and spoke with her. She told Bernadette that she should pray for sinners and do penance. The Lady also told her to have a chapel built there in her honor.

Many people did not believe Bernadette when she spoke of her vision. She had to suffer very much. But one day Our Lady told Bernadette to dig in the mud. As she did, a spring of water began to flow. The next day it continued to grow larger and larger. Many miracles happened when people began to use this water.

When Bernadette was older, she became a sister. She was always very humble. More than anything else, she desired not to be praised. She did not want to receive special treatment just because she had actually seen the Blessed Virgin. Although her own health was poor, she helped care for the sick and elderly sisters. She died in 1879 at the age of thirty-six. Her last words were: "Holy Mary, Mother of God, pray for me, a poor sinner." She was proclaimed a saint by Pope Pius XI on December 8, 1933.

We can become close to Mary as Bernadette was by reciting the Rosary every day. We could offer the Rosary for many intentions, especially for the conversion of people who are caught in sin and addictions.

FEBRUARY 19

ST. BARBATUS

Barbatus was born in Benevento, Italy, in 612. He was given a Christian upbringing and was good and devout. He took his faith seriously and especially liked to read the Bible. As soon as he was old enough, he was ordained a priest. Later he was made a pastor. But his life as a pastor was not easy. Some people did not like him to tell them how to live. St. Barbatus was encouraging them to lead better lives. He reminded them to be sorry for their sins. Some of the people were angry. They persecuted him and finally forced him to leave.

The young priest felt bad. He went back to Benevento where he had been born. He was received with great joy. There were challenges in that city, too. Many converts to Christianity still kept pagan idols in their homes. They found it hard to destroy their good luck charms. They believed in magic powers. St. Barbatus preached against such superstitions. But the people hung on to their false gods. The saint warned them that because of this sin, their city would be attacked by enemies and it was.

Afterward, the people gave up their error and peace returned. St. Barbatus was made bishop. He continued his work to convert his people. He died on February 29, 682, at the age of seventy.

Our parish priests, like St. Barbatus, want us to be good so that we will go to heaven. Let us listen to their advice and follow it.

FEBRUARY 20

ST. EUCHERIUS

St. Eucherius was born in Orleans, France, in the eighth century. He received a Christian upbringing and education. A sentence from Paul's first letter to the Corinthians made a big impression on him: "This world as we see it is passing away" (1 Corinthians 7:31). It made Eucherius realize that our lives on this earth are very short. He realized that heaven and hell last forever. He decided to seek the joys of heaven by living for God alone.

In 714, St. Eucherius left his rich home and entered a Benedictine abbey. There he spent seven years in close union with God. After the death of his uncle, the bishop of Orleans, in 721, Eucherius was chosen to take his place. Eucherius was then only twenty-five and he was very humble. He did not want to leave his beloved abbey. With tears, he begged to be allowed to remain alone with God in the monastery. But finally, he gave in for love of obedience. Eucherius became a holy, wise bishop. He did much good to his priests and people.

A powerful political figure, Charles Martel,

used to take some of the Church's money to support his wars. Because Bishop Eucherius told him that was wrong, Charles had him taken prisoner. He was exiled first to Cologne, then to a fort near Liege. But the governor in whose charge Martel had placed the bishop was moved by Eucherius' meekness toward his enemies. Some time later, the governor quietly released the bishop from prison and sent him to a monastery. Here the saint spent all his time peacefully in prayer until his death in 743.

Let us think about Paul's good advice to the Corinthians that this world of ours is passing away. This will help us to think more of our eternal goal: heaven.

FEBRUARY 21

ST. PETER DAMIAN

St. Peter Damian was born in 1007, and was left an orphan as a little child. He was taken in by an older brother who abused and starved him. Another brother named Damian became aware of the boy's real situation. He brought him to his own home. It was then that Peter's life took on a whole new direction. He was treated with love, affection and care. So grateful was he that when he became a religious he took the name Damian after his loving brother. Damian educated Peter and encouraged his studies. Peter eventually taught at the university while he was in his twenties. He was thought of as a great teacher. But the Lord was directing him in ways he could never have thought of.

Peter lived in times when many in the Church were too influenced by secular goals. Peter realized that the Church is divine and has the grace from Jesus to save all people. He wanted the Church to shine with the holiness of Jesus. After seven years of teaching, he made the decision to become a monk. He wanted to live the rest of his life in prayer and penance. He would pray and sacrifice so that many people in the Church would become holy. He went to a monastery of St. Romuald. Peter Damian wrote a rule for the monks. He also wrote a life of their holy founder, Romuald. Peter wrote many works of theology to help people deepen their faith. Twice his abbot sent him to neighboring monasteries. He helped the monks begin reforms that would encourage them to live closer to God. The monks were grateful because Peter was so kind and respectful.

Peter was finally called from the monastery. He became a bishop and a cardinal. He was sent on very important missions for various popes throughout his long life. St. Peter Damian died in 1072 at the age of eighty-three. Because he was a champion of truth and a peacemaker, he was declared a Doctor of the Church in 1828. The poet Dante (who lived from 1265 to 1321) recognized the greatness of St. Peter Damian. In his poem, the "Divine Comedy," Dante places

Damian in the "seventh heaven." That was his place for holy people who loved to think about or contemplate God.

Several years of St. Peter Damian's childhood were sad and unfortunate. But he learned how to find the Lord with childlike trust. He used his gifts to make Jesus and his Church more loved and appreciated. We can ask St. Peter Damian to show us how to live generously for God.

FEBRUARY 22

CHAIR OF ST. PETER

St. Peter was the prince of the apostles and the first pope. Jesus said to him, "You are Peter, and on this rock I will build my church" (Matthew 16:18). After Jesus went back to heaven, St. Peter preached the Gospel. He guided the small but growing Christian community. At first, Peter labored in Jerusalem and in Antioch, two big cities of the east. Later, he went to preach the Gospel in Rome, the capital of the world.

What chance did Peter have to perform his great task for the Lord? His Master had been crucified but then had risen. Who would believe that? The evils of pagan Rome would drown his voice no matter how dedicated he may be. But the Holy Spirit was alive in Peter. He courageously took up the ministry Jesus had left him. Never again would

Peter deny his Lord. Never again would Peter put his own personal well-being before the good of the Church.

The feast of St. Peter's Chair at Rome reminds us that St. Peter started the Christian community in that city. The special chair is a symbol of the authority that was given to him by Jesus. Kings of old sat on thrones and ruled. Peter's chair is a symbol of his authority from Jesus to rule the Church.

St. Peter was martyred for the faith, but down through the ages there has always been a bishop of Rome. He is the pope. The pope rules the whole Church, as St. Peter did, in Jesus' name. We call the successor of St. Peter the Holy Father.

We love and honor the pope. He takes the place of Jesus on earth. Let us always pray for our Holy Father. We ask that God may give him strength, light and comfort.

FEBRUARY 23

ST. POLYCARP

Polycarp was born between the years 75 and 80. He became a Christian when the followers of Jesus were still few. In fact, Polycarp was a disciple of one of the original apostles, St. John. All that Polycarp learned from St. John he taught to others. Polycarp became a priest and then bishop of Smyrna in present-day Turkey. He was Smyrna's bishop for many years. The Christians recognized him as a holy, brave shepherd.

Christians in Polycarp's time faced persecution and death under Emperor Marcus Aurelius. Someone betrayed Polycarp to the authorities. When his captors came to arrest him, he invited them first to share a meal with him. Then he asked them to let him pray a while. The judge tried to force Bishop Polycarp to save himself from death by cursing Jesus. "I have served Jesus all my life," answered the saint, "and he has never done me any wrong. How can I curse my King who died for me?"

The soldiers tied St. Polycarp's hands behind his back. The old bishop was then placed on a burning pile. But the fire did not harm him. One of the soldiers then stabbed a lance into his heart. And so, in the year 155, Polycarp died a martyr. He went to be forever with the Divine Master he had served so bravely.

Polycarp was called upon to stand with Jesus even at the cost of his life. We might not have to give up our lives as martyrs for Jesus. We do know, though, that we will have to make the right daily choices if we want to be the kind of Christian Polycarp was. Our choices will involve the television and videos we watch, the music we listen to, the magazines and books we read. Our choices will also determine the kind of language we use, the way we treat our family, relatives, neighbors and friends. What kind of Christians will we be?

ST. MONTANUS, ST. LUCIUS AND COMPANIONS

Emperor Valerian persecuted Christians with vengeance during the days of the early Church. He had permitted St. Cyprian's execution in September 258. The Roman official who had actually sentenced Cyprian died himself soon after. The new official, Solon, was nearly the victim of an uprising which included a plot on his life. It seems he suspected the plot to be in revenge for the death of St. Cyprian. He arrested eight innocent people. All were Christians; most were clergy. Each had been a devoted follower of St. Cyprian.

The Christians were taken down into dark dungeons. They found others there whom they knew. The filth and dampness circled the group. They realized that they would soon be facing death and eternity. The Christians were kept many months in the prison. They worked during the day and often were denied food and water without any reason. Somehow in such inhuman conditions, the little Christian community bonded and helped one another. The lay people protected the bishops, priests and deacons who were especially targets of the emperor's cruelty.

When the Christians were finally called to the place of execution, each was permitted to speak.

Montanus, who was tall and strong, spoke bravely to all the Christian crowd. He told them to be true to Jesus and to die rather than give up the faith. Lucius, who was small and frail, walked quietly to the place of execution. He was weak from the harsh months in prison. In fact, he had to lean on two friends who helped him arrive at the spot where the executioner waited. The people who watched called to him to remember them from paradise.

As each of the Christians were beheaded one after another, the crowd became more and more courageous. They wept for those who suffered such injustice. But they were joyful, too. They realized that these martyrs would bless them from heaven. Montanus, Lucius and their companions were martyred in 259.

The early Christians were known for the kindness and love they had for one another. They put the needs of others before their own and tried with all their hearts to overcome selfishness. We might be able to think of some times in our own lives when we can be more generous and less selfish in imitation of the first Christians.

ST. CAESARIUS OF NAZIANZEN

Caesarius lived in the fourth century in present-day Turkey. His father was the bishop of Nazianzen. At that time bishops and priests could marry. Caesarius' brother is St. Gregory of Nazianzen, the close friend of St. Basil. Besides being a saint, Gregory is an important writer from the early Church. His books are still read today.

Both Caesarius and Gregory received an excellent education. But while Gregory wanted to be a priest, Caesarius wanted to be a medical doctor. Both went to the schools that would help them accomplish their goals.

Caesarius completed his studies in medicine at Constantinople. He soon became a well-known and trusted physician. In fact, Emperor Constantius, who lived in Constantinople, wanted Caesarius to be his personal physician. Caesarius thanked the emperor but gently refused. He wanted to go back to Nazianzen, his home city.

Some time later, however, Caesarius was again called to serve the emperor at Constantinople. This time it was the man known to history as Julian the apostate. An apostate was someone who gave up his Christian faith. This man had several official orders against the Christians. He was willing to exempt Caesarius, however, since he was such a good doctor. Julian tried to coax the doctor into giving up his faith. Caesarius was offered positions, bribes and privileges. Caesarius' father and brother advised him to refuse the offers. They suggested he return home to practice medicine.

In 368, Caesarius was almost killed in an earthquake. He escaped unharmed but was badly shaken by the incident. He felt that God was telling him to live a life of prayer away from the noise and flattery of the court. Caesarius gave away his possessions to the poor. He began to live a quiet, prayerful life.

St. Caesarius died shortly after in 369. The homily at his funeral was preached by his brother, St. Gregory.

We all have a particular calling in life. God has given us the gifts to perform that calling well. Like St. Caesarius, we need the wisdom to listen to people we trust. We also need to refuse to follow people who want to use our talents or education in wrong ways.

FEBRUARY 26

ST. PORPHYRY

Porphyry was born in the fifth century to wealthy, noble parents. He left his family when he was twenty-five. Porphyry went to Egypt to enter a monastery. After five years, he made a trip to Jerusalem. He wanted to visit the places where Jesus had actually been while he was on earth.

Porphyry was very impressed by the Holy Land. His love for Jesus made him more deeply aware of the sufferings of the poor. At home in Thessalonica he had never known what it was like to be poor. Now he still owned all that his parents had left him. But not for long. He asked his friend Mark to go to Thessalonica and sell everything for him. After three months, Mark returned with the money. Porphyry then gave it away to those who really needed it.

At the age of forty he became a priest and was given care of the relics of the true cross of Jesus. Porphyry was then made bishop of Gaza. He worked generously to lead the people to believe in Jesus and to accept the faith. But his labors were slow and required heroic patience. The majority of inhabitants at that time were locked into pagan practices and superstitions. Although Porphyry was able to stop many of these practices, he had enemies who made him suffer greatly.

Others who were Christians loved and admired him deeply. They prayed and sacrificed for him. They begged the Lord to preserve him. Bishop Porphyry spent many years strengthening the Christian community. He proclaimed all that Christianity stood for. He died in 420.

This saint's example challenges us to have nothing to do with foolish superstitions. There is no such thing as good luck from charms and other such things. God watches over us and gives us all the help we need, if we ask him.

ST. GABRIEL OF
OUR LADY OF SORROWS

This lovable saint was born in Assisi, Italy, in 1838. He received the name Francis at Baptism, in honor of the great St. Francis of Assisi. His mother died when he was only four. Francis' father sent for a governess to raise him and the other children.

Francis grew to be very handsome and likable. He was often the most popular person at a party. He loved to have fun but there was another side to him, too. Even while having good times, he was sometimes bored. He couldn't explain why. He seemed to feel in his heart a strong desire for God and the deeper things of life.

Twice he became so sick he nearly died. Each time he promised Our Lady that if she would obtain his cure, he would become a religious. He did get better both times, but he did not keep his promise.

One day, he saw a picture of the Sorrowful Mother that was being carried in a procession. It seemed that the Blessed Mother was looking straight at him. At the same time, he heard a voice in his heart telling him, "Francis, the world is not for you anymore."

That did it. Francis entered the Passionist monastery. He was eighteen. The name he took was Gabriel of the Sorrowful Mother.

Gabriel's great loves became the Holy Eucharist and Mary, the Sorrowful Mother. He loved to spend time thinking about the passion of Jesus and how much the Lord had suffered for him. Gabriel also learned to practice two virtues in a special way: humility and obedience. His special trademark was joy. He was always happy and spread that happiness to those around him. After only four years in the Passionist order, Gabriel died on February 27, 1862. He was proclaimed a saint by Pope Benedict XV in 1920.

We should not think only of having good times. We can ask St. Gabriel to help us find real joy and meaning in our life.

❧

FEBRUARY 28

ST. ROMANUS AND ST. LUPICINUS

These French saints were brothers who lived in the fifth century. As a youth, St. Romanus was admired by everyone for his goodness. He had a great desire to become a saint. Since he saw that in the world it was too easy to forget about God, Romanus decided to live as a hermit. First, he asked the advice of a holy monk, and then he started off. He took a book with him. It was *The Lives of the Fathers of the Desert* by Cassian. He also took seeds to plant and a few tools. With these supplies, he went into the forests of the Jura mountains between Switzerland and France. Romanus found a huge fir tree and settled beneath it. He spent his time praying and reading his book. He also planted and cared for his garden, quietly enjoying nature.

Soon afterward, his brother Lupicinus joined him. Romanus and Lupicinus were very different. Romanus was hard on himself. However, he was kind and gentle and full of understanding with others. Lupicinus was hard and severe with himself and usually the same with others. Yet he meant well. The two brothers understood each other and got along fine.

Many men came to join them. They wanted to be monks, too, so they built two monasteries. Romanus was the abbot of one and Lupicinus was the abbot of the other. The monks lived simple, hard lives. They prayed much and made sacrifices cheerfully. They performed penances to strengthen themselves in their vocation. They worked very hard farming to grow their food and kept silent all the time. They chose to live like this because their main concern was growing close to God. Their lifestyle helped them toward their spiritual goal.

St. Romanus died in 460. His younger brother, St. Lupicinus, died in 480.

St. Romanus and St. Lupicinus were both saints, even though they had different personalities. We can learn from these two saints that we all have gifts and qualities that we can use to bring people closer to God. What the Lord looks for is our willingness.

march

ST. FELIX II

This pope is an ancestor of the future Pope St. Gregory the Great who lived from 540 to 604. Gregory wrote that when his aunt, St. Tharsilla, was dying, Pope Felix appeared to her. He beckoned her to heaven. Who was Pope St. Felix? And what events unfolded in his life that had led him to sainthood?

Although there are not many details, we know that Felix was a Roman. He was honest and courageous in troubled times. Felix became pope in 483. Groups of people within the Church were divided because of false teachings. Political factors complicated the ministry of this pope. But Felix proved himself a brave defender of the truths of our faith and the rights of the Church. Many compared him to Pope St. Leo the Great who had died in 461. Pope Felix was truly universal in outlook. He tried to grasp and solve the problems of the Church in various parts of the world.

Felix spent nine years of his life as pope. He will be remembered as totally dedicated to Jesus and his Church. Pope St. Felix died in 492.

We all find soon enough that life has its share of responsibilities. Sometimes we might think we want to be free of anyone or anything that can tie us down. Then we can pray to St. Felix and ask him for the generosity and courage to be faithful to our commitments.

MARCH 2

BLESSED CHARLES THE GOOD

Count Charles of Flanders, was called "the good" by the people of his kingdom. They named him for what they found him to truly be. He was the son of St. Canute, king of Denmark. Charles was just five years old when his father was murdered in 1086. When Charles grew up, he married a good young woman named Margaret. Charles was a mild and fair ruler. The people trusted him and his laws. He tried to be an example of what he expected the people to be.

Some nobles accused Charles of unjustly favoring the poor over the rich. He answered kindly, "It is because I am so aware of the needs of the poor and the pride of the rich." The poor of his realm were fed daily at his castles.

Charles ordered the abundant planting of crops so that the people would have plenty to eat at reasonable prices. Some wealthy men tried to hoard grain to sell at very high prices. Charles the Good found out and forced them to sell immediately and at fair prices. An influential father and his sons had been reprimanded by Charles for their violent tactics. They joined the little group of enemies who now wanted to kill him.

The count walked every morning barefoot to Mass and arrived early at the Church of St. Donatian. He did this in a spirit of penance. He longed to deepen his own spiritual life with God. His enemies knew that he walked to church and also that he prayed often alone before Mass. Many people who loved Charles feared for his life. They warned him that his walks to St. Donatian could lead to his death. He replied, "We are always in the middle of dangers, but we belong to God." One morning, as he prayed alone before the statue of Mary, his attackers killed him. Charles was martyred in 1127.

If we want to make a difference in this world, we can imitate Blessed Charles. He let his love for Jesus influence his daily life. When he left the church each morning, he really set out to "live the Mass." We can ask him to help us do the same.

MARCH 3

BLESSED KATHARINE DREXEL

Blessed Katharine was born in Philadelphia, Pennsylvania, on November 26, 1858. Katharine's mother died when she was a baby. Her father married a wonderful woman named Emma. She

raised their own child, Louise. She was also a loving mother to Mr. Drexel's two little girls by his former marriage. They were Elizabeth and Katharine. The girls had a wonderful childhood. Even though their family was wealthy, they were taught to be loving toward their neighbors. They were taught to be especially concerned about the poor. This was how they could show their love for God.

When Katharine grew up, she was a very active Catholic. She was generous with her time and her money. She realized that the Church had many needs. She turned her energies and her fortune to the poor, the forgotten. Her work for Jesus would be among the African American and Native American people. In 1891, Katharine began a new religious community of missionaries. They were called the Sisters of the Blessed Sacrament. Katharine would become known as Mother Katharine.

The sisters of her order center their life around Jesus in the Eucharist. They devote their love and talents to African and Native Americans. Mother Katharine inherited her family's fortune. She poured the money into wonderful works of charity. She and her sisters started schools, convents and missionary churches. In 1925, they established Xavier University in New Orleans. During her long, fruitful lifetime, Mother Katharine spent millions of dollars of the Drexel fortune for the wonderful works that she and her sisters accomplished for the poor. She believed that she found Jesus truly present in the Eucharist. So, too, she found him in the African and Native Americans whom she lovingly served.

Mother Katharine died on March 3, 1955, at the age of ninety-seven. She was declared "blessed" by Pope John Paul II on November 20, 1988.

Mother Katharine teaches us a valuable lesson. We can spend our lives looking after ourselves and our own comfort. How much better, though, to be like Mother Katharine Drexel. This way we can do as much as we can to help others.

MARCH 4

ST. CASIMIR

St. Casimir was born in 1458, son of Casimir IV, king of Poland. Casimir was one of thirteen children. With the help of his virtuous mother and his dedicated teacher, Casimir received an excellent education.

When he was thirteen, Casimir had the chance to become king of neighboring Hungary, but he refused. He spent the rest of his life trying to live his Christian ideals. He went out of his way to be cheerful and friendly with everybody. Beneath the surface of his busy life, he made the effort to help himself to grow spiritually. He often fasted and slept on the floor of his room as penance. He prayed daily, sometimes even during the middle of the night. He loved to think and pray about the passion of Jesus. He recognized this as a good way to learn to love God. Casimir also loved the Blessed Virgin Mary with a special love. In her honor, he recited a beautiful hymn very often. The name of the hymn is "Daily, Daily, Sing to Mary." His hand-written copy of it was buried with him.

Casimir was never healthy, yet he was courageous and strong in character. He would always do what he knew was right. Sometimes he would even advise his father, the king, to rule the people fairly. He always did this with great respect and his father listened to him.

St. Casimir had a great love and respect for virginity. His parents found a very beautiful and virtuous young woman for him to marry. However, Casimir chose to give his heart to God alone. While in Lithuania on an assignment of service for that country, Casimir became ill with tuberculosis. He died at the age of twenty-six. He was proclaimed a saint by Pope Leo X in 1521.

St. Casimir helps us see that even if our bodies are not strong or healthy, we can still be strong in character. We can always stand up for what is right, but in a kind way.

ST. JOHN JOSEPH OF THE CROSS

St. John Joseph of the Cross was born in southern Italy on the feast of the Assumption, 1654. He was a young noble, but he dressed like a poor man. He did that because he wanted to be as poor as Jesus had been.

At the age of sixteen, John Joseph entered the Franciscan order. He wanted very much to live a self-sacrificing life as Jesus had. This led him to cheerfully make many sacrifices. He slept just three hours a night and ate very plain food.

Later he was ordained a priest. Father John Joseph became the superior at Santa Lucia's in Naples where he spent most of his long life. He always insisted on doing the hardest work. He cheerfully chose to do the duties that no one else wanted.

St. John Joseph had a very loving nature. But he did not try to be the center of attention. Instead of waiting for people to recognize his gifts and reach out to him, he would reach out to others. All the priests and brothers thought of him as a loving father. He greatly loved the Blessed Virgin, too, and tried to help others love her.

This good priest loved God so much that even when he was sick, he kept on working. St. John Joseph died on March 6, 1734, at the age of eighty. He was proclaimed a saint by Pope Pius VIII in 1839.

St. John Joseph was generous with his love for God and people. He invites us to overcome the selfishness that holds us back in our journey to God. Let us make it a point to treat everyone with equal respect and kindness, even if we might like some people better than others.

MARCH 6

ST. COLETTE

Born in 1380, Nicolette was named in honor of St. Nicholas of Myra. Her loving parents nick-named her Colette from the time she was a baby. Colette's father was a carpenter at an abbey in Picardy. Quiet and hard-working, Colette was a big help to her mother with the housework. Her parents noticed the child's liking for prayer and her sensitive, loving nature.

When Colette was seventeen, both her parents died. The young woman was placed under the care of the abbot at the monastery where her father had worked. She asked for and received a hut built next to the abbey church. Colette lived there. She spent her time praying and sacrificing for Jesus' Church. More and more people found out about this holy young woman. They went to see her and asked her advice about important problems. They knew that she was wise because she lived close to God. She received everybody with gentle kindness. After each visit, she would pray that her visitors would find peace of soul.

Colette was a member of the Third Order of St. Francis. She knew that the religious order of women who followed St. Francis' lifestyle are the Poor Clares. They are named after St. Clare, their foundress, who was a follower of St. Francis. During Colette's time, the Poor Clares needed to go back to the original purpose of their order. St. Francis of Assisi appeared to Colette and asked her to reform the Poor Clares. She must have been surprised and afraid of such a difficult task. But she trusted in God's grace. Colette traveled to the Poor Clare convents. She helped the nuns become more poor and prayerful.

The Poor Clares were inspired by St. Colette's life. She had a great devotion to Jesus in the Eucharist. She also spent time frequently meditating on the passion and death of Jesus. She loved Jesus and her religious vocation very much.

Colette knew exactly when and where she was going to die. She died in one of her convents in Ghent, Flanders, in 1447. She was sixty-seven. Colette was proclaimed a saint by Pope Pius VI in 1807.

St. Colette teaches us that even if what we are asked to do is hard, we can find joy just the same. We can do this by keeping in close touch each day with God.

ST. PERPETUA AND ST. FELICITY

Perpetua and Felicity lived in Carthage, North Africa, in the third century. It was the time of the fierce persecution of Christians by Emperor Septimus Severus.

Twenty-two-year-old Perpetua was the daughter of a rich nobleman. While growing up, she had received everything she wanted. But she realized that she loved Jesus and her Christian faith more than anything the world could offer. For this she found herself a prisoner on the way to execution.

Perpetua's father was a pagan. He did everything possible to persuade his daughter to give up her Christian faith. He tried to convince her of the importance of saving her life. But the woman would not give in, even though she knew that she would have to leave behind her husband and baby.

Felicity, Perpetua's Christian maid, had been a slave. She and Perpetua were great friends. They shared their belief in and love for Jesus. Felicity, too, was willing to sacrifice her life for Jesus and for her faith. For this she also found herself a prisoner on the way to execution.

Felicity was also a young wife. While in prison for her faith, she became a mother as well. Her little baby was adopted by a good Christian woman. Felicity was happy because now she could die a martyr.

Hand in hand, Perpetua and Felicity bravely faced martyrdom together. They were charged by wild animals and then beheaded. They died around the year 202.

The martyrs were so faithful to Christ that they made great sacrifices. They even gave up their lives for him. Let us ask Perpetua and Felicity to help us make cheerfully the little sacrifices that come our way.

❦

MARCH 8

ST. JOHN OF GOD

St. John was born in Portugal on March 8, 1495. His parents were poor, but deeply Christian. John was a restless boy. For a while he was a shepherd, then a soldier, then a storekeeper. During his adult years he was not religious. He and his friends had lost any awareness of God. By the time John was forty, he began to feel empty. He was sad about the life he was wasting away. In church he heard a homily by the holy missionary, John of Avila. The impact of his life hit John of God. He began to weep right out loud. During the days ahead, St. John of Avila helped John begin his life again with hope and courage.

John of God began to live differently. He put prayer and penance into his daily life. It is believed that a bishop gave John his name because he changed his selfish life completely and truly became "of God." Gradually, John of God realized how much poverty and suffering filled the lives of people. He began to spend his time nursing the sick in the hospitals and asylums. Then he realized sadly that many people were too poor to have hospital care. Who would take care of them? He decided that, for the love of God, he would.

When he was forty-five, John obtained a house for the care of the sick poor. The house became a small hospital where every person in need was welcomed. Those who came to help John gradually formed a religious order for the care of the poor. They are called Brothers of St. John of God.

Some people must have wondered if John was as holy as he seemed. Once, a marquis disguised himself as a beggar. He knocked on John's door, asking for alms. John cheerfully gave him everything he had, which amounted to a few dollars. The marquis did not reveal his identity at the time but went away very impressed. The next day a messenger arrived at John's door with a letter of explanation and his money returned. In addition, the marquis sent 150 gold crowns. He also had fresh bread, meat and eggs delivered every morning to the hospital—enough for all the patients and staff.

After ten years of hard work in his hospital, St. John became sick himself. He died on his birthday in 1550. John of God was proclaimed a saint by Blessed Pope Innocent XI in 1690.

St. John of God listened to the advice of St. John of Avila and other spiritual people. They helped him make good choices. We all need the good advice of people we trust.

The current Roman calendar offers St. Frances of Rome today. Because this book is for young people, we have also added the popular St. Dominic Savio, whose feast was celebrated on March 9 in the previous calendar of saints.

☙❦❧

ST. FRANCES OF ROME

St. Frances was born in 1384. Her parents were wealthy, but they taught Frances to be concerned about people and to live a good Christian life. She was an intelligent little girl. Frances informed her parents when she was eleven that she had made up her mind to be a nun. Her parents encouraged her to think of marriage instead. As was the custom, they selected a good young man to be Frances' husband. The bride was just thirteen.

Frances and her husband, Lorenzo Ponziano, fell in love with each other. Even though their marriage was arranged, they were happily married for forty years. Lorenzo admired his wife and his sister-in-law, Vannozza. Both women prayed every day and performed penances for Jesus' Church, which had many trials at that time. Frances and Vannozza also visited the poor. They took care of the sick. They brought food and firewood to people who needed it. Other wealthy women were inspired by their example to do more with their lives too. All the while, Frances became more and more prayerful. She really grew close to Jesus and Mary in her everyday life.

Frances and Lorenzo were compassionate people. They knew what it was like to suffer. They lost two of their three children from the plague. This made them even more sensitive to the needs of the poor. During the wars between the legitimate pope and the anti-popes, Lorenzo led the armies that defended the true pope. While he was away at battle, his enemies destroyed his property and possessions. Even then, Frances cleaned up a part of the family villa that had been wrecked and used it for a hospital. As hard as things were for her family, the people out on the street were in greater need. Lorenzo was wounded and came home to be nursed back to health by his loving wife. He died in 1436. Frances spent the remaining four years of her life in the religious congregation she helped to start.

St. Frances of Rome died on March 9, 1440. She was declared a saint by Pope Paul V in 1608.

Frances truly loved Jesus and his Church. She knew that the best way to show that love was to pray for the Church. Other ways were to take good care of her family and to look after the interests of the poor. We, too, can ask St. Frances to help us know how to show our love for Jesus and his Church.

ST. DOMINIC SAVIO

St. Dominic Savio was born in northern Italy in 1842. One day when he was just four, he disappeared and his mother went to look for him. Dominic was in a quiet corner on his knees, hands joined in prayer. At five, he was an altar boy. When he was seven, he received his First Holy Communion. On that day, Dominic chose a motto for himself. He promised Jesus in his heart, "Death, but not sin!" And he prayed every day to be true to his promise.

When he was twelve, Dominic went to the school run by St. John Bosco in Turin, Italy. Dominic missed his family, but he was happy to be at Don Bosco's school. Here he would learn everything that he would need to become a priest. That was his great goal—to become a priest. He was a good student, but fun, too. He was the kind of person Don Bosco and the students knew they could depend on.

Once Dominic broke up a fight between two angry boys. He was armed only with a crucifix. Another time, Dominic noticed a group of bigger boys huddled in a circle. He worked his way through to see what was so interesting and found pornographic magazines. He grabbed them and ripped them up. The boys had never seen Dominic so angry. "Oh, what's so wrong with looking at these pictures anyway?" one of the boys blurted. "If you don't see anything wrong," Dominic said sadly, "this is even worse. It means you're used to looking at dirty things!"

Dominic began to feel sick. He was sent home to his family to get better. But even in his hometown, his health did not improve. He grew worse instead and received the last sacraments. He began to realize that he would not be going back to Don Bosco's school. His great hope of becoming a priest was not to be. Just before he died, he tried to sit up. He said to his father, "I am seeing wonderful things." He rested his head on the pillow and closed his eyes. Dominic died in 1857; he was fifteen years old.

We can make many wonderful plans and set great goals for our life. But Dominic Savio reminds us that we don't know how long we have on this earth. He never did become a priest, but he became a saint. That is because he tried his best to live by the motto he set for himself: "Death, but not sin." We can ask Dominic to help us live his motto, too.

MARCH 10

ST. SIMPLICIUS

St. Simplicius became pope in 468. Sometimes it seemed to him that he was all alone in trying to correct evils that were everywhere. Conquerers had taken over vast territories. Even Rome itself was occupied by invaders. The people were hungry and poor. They had been taxed and robbed by former Roman officials. Poverty prowled the streets and removed all joy. The new Conquerers at least had not asked for taxes. Pope Simplicius tried in every way to uplift his people and to work for their good. He was always there for them, no matter how small his efforts seemed to him. And because he was holy, he never gave up. More than by words, he taught with the example of his holy life.

St. Simplicius had to suffer greatly as pope for another reason as well. Some of his own Christians stubbornly held on to their wrong opinions. Then with great sorrow, St. Simplicius had to put them out of the Church. When he corrected people who were doing wrong, he was kind and humble.

Simplicius was pope for fifteen years and eleven months. Then the Lord called him to receive the reward of his labors. St. Simplicius died in 483 and was buried in St. Peter's Basilica in Rome.

From St. Simplicius we are reminded that taking responsibility requires courage. Not everything in life will happen the way we might like it. We can learn to accept unpleasant or painful circumstances as opportunities to grow. It will seem that some people deliberately put obstacles to block the good things we do. Then we can pray to St. Simplicius. We can ask him to help us be like him and never give up.

MARCH 11

ST. EULOGIUS OF SPAIN

St. Eulogius lived in the ninth century. His family was well-known and he received an excellent education. While he learned his lessons, he also learned from the good example of his teachers. Eulogius loved to read about and study the Bible. His Bible-reading helped him love the Word of God. He wanted to bring God's message to everyone. When he grew up, he became a priest and the head of a famous school.

At this time the Muslims had taken over Spain. They were opposed to Christianity. At first they tried to make the people give up their faith. When the people refused to change their religion, they were put in prison. Some were even killed.

Eulogius and his bishop were put in prison along with many other Christians. In the prison, Eulogius read the Bible out loud to encourage the prisoners. As they listened, they no longer felt afraid to die for Jesus. During this time, St. Eulogius wrote a book encouraging Christians to die rather than give up their holy faith.

The saint himself wanted to be a martyr more than anything else. Instead, he was let out of prison. As soon as he was free, St. Eulogius began to preach and he converted many. His former captors were so angry that they arrested him again. In front of the judge, he bravely declared that Jesus is God. Eulogius was condemned and offered his life for Jesus. He died in 859.

We are proud of our country's war heroes. We dream of doing the great deeds they did. St. Eulogius' life reminds us that we can be very proud of the heroes of our faith, too. We can try to be like them.

MARCH 12

ST. FINA (SERAPHINA)

Fina was born in a little Italian town called San Geminiano. Her parents had once been well off, but misfortune had left them poor. Seraphina, or Fina, as her family called her, was their daughter. Fina was pretty and lively. She had a generous nature. Each day she saved half of her dinner for someone in the town poorer than she. During the day she sewed and spun cloth to help pay the family debts. At night, she usually spent a long time praying to Jesus and Mary.

When she was still quite young, her father died. Fina was struck with an illness that deformed and paralyzed her. Movement became almost impossible and Fina lay for six years on wooden planks. Pain rushed through her whole body. The only way she could bear it was to concentrate on Jesus as he was nailed to the cross. "I unite my sufferings to yours, Jesus," she would whisper. Sometimes, when the pain was horrible, she would say, "It is not my wounds but yours, O Christ, that hurt me." Fina was left alone for many hours every day because her mother had to go out to work or beg. The neighbors knew about Fina, but her sores had become so foul-smelling that people made excuses for not going to visit her.

Unexpectedly, Fina's mother passed away. Now the girl was left alone. Only one neighbor, her good friend Beldia, came to care for her. Beldia tried to give Fina as much attention as she could, but Fina was usually left alone. It was obvious that she could not live much longer. She refused to lose heart. Someone mentioned to her about the tremendous sufferings St. Gregory the Great had endured. Fina became devoted to him. It is said that one day, as she groaned in pain, St. Gregory appeared to her. He said kindly, "Child, on my feast day God will grant you rest." His feast day in older calendars had been celebrated on March 12, because he had died on March 12, 604. So on March 12, 1253, St. Gregory came to take Fina home to heaven.

St. Fina helps us appreciate the Christian meaning and value of suffering. We can also realize the value of visiting shut-ins, the elderly, the ill. We can ask St. Fina to give us a sensitive heart for people who are lonely or suffering.

MARCH 13

ST. EUPHRASIA

St. Euphrasia was born in the fifth century to deeply Christian parents. Her father, a relative of the emperor, died when she was a year old. The emperor looked after her mother and her. When the girl was seven, her mother took her to Egypt. There they lived in a large house near a convent of nuns. Euphrasia was fascinated by the nuns. She begged her mother to let her serve God in the convent in which the holy nuns lived. She was just a little girl, but she wasn't about to give up the idea or forget her request. Soon after, Euphrasia's mother took her to the convent and put her in the care of the abbess.

Years passed. When Euphrasia's mother died, the emperor reminded the young woman that her parents had promised her in marriage to a rich young senator. Of course Euphrasia wanted to belong to no one but Jesus. So she wrote a respectful letter to the emperor. In it she said, "I belong to Jesus, and I cannot give myself to anyone else. My only desire is that the world should forget about me completely. I humbly beg Your Majesty to take all the riches my parents left me and give them to the poor. I ask Your Majesty to free all the slaves of my family. Please cancel all the debts people owe me." The emperor thought her letter was so beautiful that he read it out loud to all the senators. Then he did everything she had asked.

Euphrasia spent the rest of her life as a nun. She never regretted that the Lord had chosen her to be a religious. Euphrasia died in 420.

It is all right to be happy with the nice clothes and many good things we have. But we should never forget that there is more to life than that. We can ask St. Euphrasia to help us appreciate people for who they are, not for what they have.

❧

MARCH 14

ST. MATILDA

St. Matilda was born about 895, the daughter of a German count. When she was still quite young, her parents arranged her marriage to a nobleman named Henry. Soon after their marriage, Henry became king of Germany.

As queen, Matilda lived a simple lifestyle with times for daily prayer. Everyone who saw her realized how good and kind she was. She was more like a mother than a queen. She loved to visit and comfort the sick. She helped prisoners. Matilda did not let herself be spoiled by her position, but tried to reach out to people in need. King Henry realized that his wife was an extraordinary person. He told her many times that he was a better person and a better king because she was his wife. Even though their marriage had been arranged, Henry and Matilda really loved each other.

Matilda was free to use the treasures of the kingdom for her charities and Henry never questioned her. In fact, he became more aware of the needs of people. He realized that he had the power to ease suffering because of his position. The couple were happily married for twenty-three years. Then King Henry died quite suddenly in 936. The queen suffered the loss very much. She decided then and there to live for God alone. So she called the priest to celebrate Mass for King Henry's soul. Then she gave the priest all the jewels she was wearing. She did this to show that she meant to give up the things of the world from then on.

Although she was a saint, Matilda made a big mistake. She favored her son, Henry, more than her son, Otto, in the struggle to be king. She was sorry for having done this. She made up for it by accepting without complaint the sufferings that came her way.

After years spent in practicing charity and penance, St. Matilda died peacefully in 968. She was buried beside her husband.

From St. Matilda we can learn to offer up little sufferings to make up for our sins and mistakes.

ST. ZACHARY

St. Zachary was a Benedictine monk from Greece who lived in the eighth century. He became a cardinal and then pope. In his time, there was fighting all over Italy. Pope St. Zachary kept making peace and saving people from terrible wars. At times he risked his life to do it.

It was because the saint was so gentle and kind that the leaders did what he asked. Even for his enemies he would do favors and give them the kindest treatment possible. He never took revenge on them. When Pope Zachary learned that the Lombards were about to attack Rome, he asked to have a meeting with their leader. The pope and Liutprand of the Lombards met. Whatever they said to each other, the results were impressive. Liutprand canceled his attack. He also returned all territory taken in that area over the previous thirty years. He even released all prisoners. Liutprand signed a twenty-year treaty in which the Romans would be guaranteed freedom from attacks from the Lombards.

St. Zachary was also known as a real father toward the poor. He built homes for the poor and for travelers. His loving heart could not bear to see people suffer. Once he heard that some businessmen had bought poor slaves in Rome and were going to sell them in Africa. He called those men and scolded them for being so cruel. Then he paid them the price they were asking for the slaves and set the slaves free.

When St. Zachary died in 752, all the people were saddened to have lost such a good and saintly father.

St. Zachary was loved and respected by everyone because he was not looking out for himself. He was concerned about the needs of everybody else. Let us ask him to show us how we can be as generous and unselfish with our lives.

MARCH 16

BLESSED TORELLO

Torello was born in 1202, in Poppi, Italy. His life as a child in the village was ordinary and uneventful. But after his father's death, Torello started to change his whole way of life. He got involved with companions who drank. They hung around town all day instead of working. Torello liked his new friends and was trying hard to win their approval.

Then while he was playing an outdoor sport one day, a rooster flew down from its roost. It landed on Torello's arm and crowed three times, long and loud. Torello was speechless. He walked away and wouldn't finish the game. He couldn't help but think that what the rooster had done was no coincidence. He was being warned, just as St. Peter had once been warned. Torello's irresponsible way of living would lead him away from Jesus.

Torello decided then and there to change his life. He went to see the abbot of San Fedele who helped him make a good confession. Then Torello went out to a quiet, wooded area and selected a spot near a big tree. He spent eight days in prayer. At the end of that time he decided that he would be a hermit. He went back to Poppi and sold all his property. He kept only enough money to buy the small square plot of land around the big tree he had found in the woods. Next to that tree he built a shack where he spent the rest of his life. He grew his own vegetables for food and got water from the stream. He prayed and performed penances, the hardest of which was sleeping only three hours a night.

Torello felt that being a hermit was what God wanted of him. This is how he peacefully spent his life. While he was alive, very few people knew of his hermit's life. Only one friend was aware of Torello's hidden life in the forest. He died at the age of eighty after spending over fifty years as a hermit. Blessed Torello died in 1282.

Blessed Torello teaches us by his life to take our eternal destiny seriously. Every human being has to die and be judged by God. The way we choose to spend our lives is the way we will spend eternity.

MARCH 17

ST. PATRICK

It is believed that St. Patrick was born in fifth-century Britain to Roman parents. When he was sixteen, he was captured by pirates and taken to Ireland. There he was sold as a slave. His owner sent him to tend his flocks on the mountains. Patrick had very little food and clothing. Yet he took good care of the animals in rain, snow and ice. Patrick was so lonely on the hillside that he turned often in prayer to Jesus and his Mother Mary. His life was hard and unfair. However, Patrick's trust in God grew stronger all the time.

Later, when he escaped from Ireland, he studied to become a priest. But Patrick always felt that he had to go back to Ireland to bring that pagan land to Christ. At last his wish came true. He became a priest and then a bishop. It was while St. Celestine I was pope that Patrick went back to Ireland. How happy he was to bring the Good News of the true God to the people who once had held him a slave.

Right from the start, Patrick suffered much. His relatives and friends wanted him to quit before the pagan Irish killed him. Yet the saint kept on preaching about Jesus. He traveled from one village to another. He seldom rested, and he

Saint Patrick

performed great penances for those people whom he so loved. Before he died, the whole nation was Christian.

Despite such great success, St. Patrick never grew proud. He called himself a poor sinner and gave all the praises to God. Patrick died in 461.

Many missionaries are laboring today to bring the Good News to our world just as Patrick did. We can pray and make sacrifices that their hard work will lead many people to belief in and love for Jesus.

❦

MARCH 18

ST. CYRIL OF JERUSALEM

Cyril was born around 315 when a new phase was beginning for Christians. Before that date, the Church was persecuted by the emperors. Thousands of Christians had been martyrs. In 315, Emperor Constantine recognized Christianity as a legal religion. That was a wonderful thing, but it didn't end all the problems. In fact, during the years that followed the Edict of 315, Christians learned about an entirely new difficulty. There was confusion about what Christians believe and don't believe. There were many false teachings called "heresies." Some priests and bishops became brave defenders of Church teaching. One such bishop was Cyril of Jerusalem.

When St. Maximus, bishop of Jerusalem, died, Cyril was chosen to take his place. Cyril was the bishop of Jerusalem for thirty-five years. Sixteen long years of that time were spent in hiding and exile. Three times he was run out of town by influential people who wanted him removed. They were trying to force Cyril to accept false teachings about Jesus and the Church. But he would not bend.

The reign of Emperor Julian the apostate began in 361. Julian decided to rebuild the famous Temple of Jerusalem. He had a definite purpose in mind: he wanted to prove that Jesus had been wrong when he declared that the Temple of Jerusalem would not be rebuilt. He decided to prove it. So he spent much money and sent all the materials for a new Temple. Many people helped by giving jewels and precious metals. Yet St. Cyril faced the difficulty with outward calm. He was sure that the Temple could not be built, because Jesus, who is God, had said so. The bishop looked calmly at all the materials and said, "I know that this will fail." And sure enough, first a storm, then an earthquake, then a fire stopped the emperor. He finally abandoned the project.

St. Cyril died in 386 when he was around seventy. This gentle, kindly man had lived in times of upheaval and sadness. But he never lost his courage because it came from Jesus. He was faithful to the Lord all his life. Cyril was heroic in teaching the truth about Jesus and his Church.

St. Cyril of Jerusalem teaches us that the Lord gives each of us opportunities to do good. We can ask St. Cyril for the courage to make our contribution no matter how great the challenge.

MARCH 19

ST. JOSEPH

St. Joseph is a great saint. He was Jesus' foster-father and Mary's husband. Joseph was given the great privilege of taking care of God's own Son, Jesus, and his Mother, Mary. Joseph was poor all his life. He had to work very hard in his carpenter shop, but he did not mind. He was happy to work for his little family. He loved Jesus and Mary so much.

Whatever the Lord wanted him to do, St. Joseph did at once, no matter how difficult it was. He was humble and pure, gentle and wise. Jesus and Mary loved him and obeyed him because God had placed him as the head of their family. What a joy for St. Joseph to live with the Son of God himself. Jesus obeyed him, helped him, and loved him.

We pray to St. Joseph as the protector of the dying for a special reason. It is believed that Joseph died peacefully in the arms of Jesus and Mary.

St. Teresa of Avila chose St. Joseph as the protector of her order of Carmelite sisters. She had a great trust in his prayers. "Every time I ask St. Joseph for something," she said, "he always obtains it for me."

Pope Pius IX proclaimed St. Joseph the patron of the Universal Church.

As Jesus obeyed and helped St. Joseph in his hard and humble work, let us, too, willingly help our parents with the work to be done at home.

❦

MARCH 20

ST. CUTHBERT

St. Cuthbert lived in England in the seventh century. He was a poor shepherd boy who loved to play games with his friends. He was very good at them, too. One of his friends scolded him for loving to play so much. In fact, his playmate said words that he didn't seem to be saying himself. The child said, "Cuthbert, how can you waste your time playing games when you have been chosen to be a priest and a bishop?" Cuthbert was confused and very impressed. He wondered if he really was going to be a priest and a bishop.

In August, 651, fifteen-year-old Cuthbert had a religious experience. He saw a totally black sky. Suddenly a bright beam of light moved across it. In the light were angels carrying a ball of fire up beyond the sky. Sometime later, Cuthbert learned that the same night of the vision, the bishop, St.

Aiden, had died. Cuthbert did not know how this all involved him, but he made up his mind about his life's vocation and entered a monastery. Cuthbert became a priest and a bishop.

From one village to another, from house to house, St. Cuthbert went, on horse or on foot. He visited the people to help them spiritually. Best of all, he could speak the dialect of the peasants because he had once been a poor shepherd boy. He did good everywhere and brought many people to God. Cuthbert was cheerful and kind. People felt attracted to him and no one was afraid of him. He was also a prayerful, holy monk.

When Cuthbert was ordained a bishop, he worked just as hard as ever to help his people. He visited them no matter how difficult the travel on poor roads or in very bad weather. As he lay dying, Cuthbert urged his monks to live in peace and charity with everyone. He died peacefully in 687.

St. Cuthbert went out of his way to be kind and loving with his people. We can ask him to help us be the same so that no one will find it hard to get along with us.

ST. SERAPION

Serapion lived in Egypt in the fourth century. Those were exciting times for the Church and for St. Serapion. As a young man, he received an impressive education in Christian theology and secular subjects. For a while, he directed the famous Christian school that taught the faith in Alexandria. Then Serapion went out into the desert and became a monk. He met the famous hermit, St. Anthony of Egypt. Serapion tried very hard to learn from and imitate him. When he died, Anthony left Serapion one of his cloaks, which he treasured for the rest of his life.

Serapion became bishop of Thmuis, a city in lower Egypt. He went to a very important meeting of bishops in Sardica in 347. Serapion proved to be a very brave bishop. He loved the truths of the faith and tried to protect them from those who wanted to change Christian beliefs. He worked with St. Athanasius, another brave bishop. Both were outstanding for their courage. They combated false teachings or heresies with their homilies and with their writings. Most of St. Serapion's writings were lost. They were letters full of instruction about the faith and an explanation of the Psalms. His most important work, called the "Euchologion," was lost for hundreds of years. It was found and published at the end of the nine-teenth century.

Another famous saint of that time, Jerome, said that Emperor Constantius sent Serapion into exile. It seems that Serapion died around the year 370 in the place where he was exiled.

St. Serapion shows us by the way he lived that being a good Christian takes courage and honesty. Often people may not understand or agree with our choices. But if we want to be true to Jesus and his Church, we will have to risk being unpopular at times. We can ask St. Serapion to give us some of his courage.

❦

MARCH 22

ST. DEOGRATIAS

The city of Carthage was taken over by barbar-ian armies in 439. The conquerors were the Vandals. They arrested the bishop and priests and put them on a large, old wooden raft and set it adrift at sea. Incredible as it may seem, they reached the port of Naples and were rescued. But the city they left behind was without a bishop for fourteen years.

Emperor Valentinian in Rome asked Genseric, the leader of the Vandals, to permit the ordination of another bishop for Carthage. Genseric agreed and a young priest of that city was chosen. He was respected by the conquerors and loved by the

Christians. His name in Latin was "Deogratias," which, in English, means "thanks be to God." Bishop Deogratias labored for the faith and well-being of the people of Carthage.

Then Genseric sacked Rome. He returned to Africa with hundreds of slaves—men, women and children. Whole families were kidnapped and divided up among the Vandals and Moors. Genseric totally disregarded natural ties. Family members were sold individually and separated from their loved ones.

Bishop Deogratias heard about the tragedy. When the slave ships docked at Carthage, he bought back as many slaves as he could. He raised the money by selling the church vessels, vestments and ornaments. He was able to free many families. He found living quarters for them. When the houses were filled up, he used two large churches for this purpose. He bought bedding and other necessary items so that the people could feel at home in their new surroundings.

Bishop Deogratias died after only three years as Carthage's bishop. He was totally worn out from his life of self-sacrifice and loving service. The people he helped would never forget him. He died in 457.

Bishop Deogratias helps us realize that we can never put a price on a human life. Each person is valuable because we are all children of God, our loving Father. We can pray to St. Deogratias so that human life will be more respected. We can especially pray for media presentations that influence people so much.

ST. TURIBIUS OF MONGROVEJO

St. Turibius was born in 1538 in Leon, Spain. He became a university professor and then a famous judge. He was a fine Christian with a reputation for being honest and wise.

An unusual thing happened to him that changed his whole life. He was asked to become the archbishop of Lima, Peru. First of all, he was not a priest. Second, Peru was in far-away South America. This happened because Lima needed an archbishop. Many people in the Church realized that Turibius had the qualities for such a trusted position. He begged to be excused from the honor. But when he learned about the miserable condition of the native people of Peru, he could not refuse. He wanted to help them and to bring them the faith. He was ordained a priest and set out for Peru.

As archbishop, St. Turibius traveled all over the country. He made his way over the snowy mountains on foot. He walked over the hot sands of the seashore. He built churches and hospitals. He started the first school in Latin America for the training of priests. Such a school is called a seminary. He learned the different native languages. He wanted the people to be able to listen to homilies at Mass and go to confession in their own language. He protected the natives who were often cruelly treated by their Conquerers.

St. Turibius loved the people of Peru. He spent the rest of his life as a priest and bishop for them. He died on March 23, 1606, at the age of sixty-eight. St. Turibius was proclaimed a saint by Pope Benedict XIII in 1726.

We don't want to be fooled into judging the importance of people by the amount of money they have or the expensive things they own. Each one is important because God is the Father of us all. We can ask St. Turibius to help us treat every person with respect and kindness as he did.

MARCH 24

BLESSED DIDACUS

Blessed Didacus Joseph was born on March 29, 1743, in Cadiz, Spain. He was baptized Joseph Francis. His parents loved their faith and practiced it. They were delighted when their child constructed an altar and decorated it. He would kneel and pray to Jesus, to Our Lady and to St. Joseph.

When he was old enough, Joseph learned how to serve Mass at the Capuchin Franciscan church just down the street. Joseph learned to love the Mass. He used to get up early enough to be at the church each morning to wait for the doors to be unlocked. He never missed a day. One of the Capuchin priests or brothers gave Joseph a book about the lives of the Capuchin saints. He read it and read it again. Joseph learned every story. He grew to love the holy men who were poor and humble like Jesus. The day came when he asked to join the order. He was accepted and went to Seville, Spain, for his training, called a novitiate. He began a new life with a new name, Brother Didacus.

After years of preparation, Brother Didacus was ordained a priest. He was sent out to preach to the people the Good News of Jesus. He loved doing this. His homilies were so clear and kind that people listened. They even brought friends to listen. Soon an ordinary church was too small for the crowds. When Father Didacus was preaching, the talks were held outdoors, usually in the town square or in the streets. Father Didacus loved to preach about the Blessed Trinity. He was always available to hear confessions, too. He was happy when people came to the sacrament of Reconciliation. Whenever he had some free time, he visited prisons and hospitals. He also would pay calls at the homes of shut-ins.

Father Didacus died in 1801 and was declared "blessed" by Pope Leo XIII in 1894.

Father Didacus lived a wonderful life for God's people. We can ask him to help us use wisely the good influences in our lives. Such influences can be holy people, religious instruction, the Mass and good books or magazines.

ANNUNCIATION OF THE LORD

The time arrived for Jesus to come down from heaven. God sent the Archangel Gabriel to the town of Nazareth where Mary lived. The glorious archangel entered Mary's little house and found her praying.

"Hail Mary, full of grace!" said the angel. "The Lord is with you, and you are blessed among women." Mary was surprised to hear the angel's words of praise.

"Do not be afraid, Mary," said Gabriel. Then he told her that she was to be the mother of Jesus, our Savior. Mary understood what a great honor God was giving her. Yet she said, "Behold the handmaid of the Lord!" At that very moment, she became the Mother of God. And still she called herself his handmaid, his servant.

Mary knew, too, that as the mother of Jesus, she would have many sorrows. She knew she would have to suffer when her Son suffered. Yet with all her heart, she said, "Be it done to me according to your word."

On this occasion, our Blessed Mother gave us a wonderful example of humility and obedience. Let us, too, show God our love by obeying those who represent him—our parents and teachers.

ST. LUDGER

St. Ludger was born in northern Europe in the eighth century. After he had studied hard for many years, he was ordained a priest. Ludger began to travel far and wide preaching the Good News. He was very happy to share all that he had learned about God with everyone who listened to him. Pagans were converted and Christians began to live much better lives. St. Ludger built many churches and monasteries.

Then suddenly barbarians called Saxons attacked his land and drove the priests out. It seemed as though all St. Ludger's work would be lost. But he would not give up. He first found a safe place for his disciples. Then he went to Rome to ask the Holy Father what he should do.

For over three years, Ludger lived in the Benedictine monastery as a good, holy monk. But he did not forget his people at home. As soon as he could get back into his country, Ludger returned and continued his work. He labored very hard and converted many of the pagan Saxons.

When he was made a bishop, Ludger gave an even better example by his great kindness and piety. Once, jealous men spoke against him to King Charlemagne. The king ordered him to come to court to defend himself. Ludger went obediently to the castle. The next day, when the king sent for him, Ludger said he would come as soon as he had finished his prayers. King Charlemagne was angry at first. But St. Ludger explained that although he had great respect for the king, he knew that God came first. "Your Majesty will not be angry with me," he said, "for you yourself have told me always to put God first." At such a wise answer, the king realized that Ludger was very holy. From then on, Charlemagne admired and loved him very much.

St. Ludger died on Passion Sunday in 809. He performed his duties in the service of God even on the day he died.

St. Ludger poured all his energy into his priestly calling. Jesus used him to bring many people closer to him. We can pray often that Jesus will help priests be as holy and generous as St. Ludger was.

❦

MARCH 27

ST. JOHN OF EGYPT

A man who desired to be alone with God was to become one of the most famous hermits of his time. St. John of Egypt was born around 304. Not much is known about his childhood except that he learned the carpenter's trade. When he was twenty-five, John decided to leave the world for good to spend his life in prayer and sacrifice for God. He was one of the famous desert hermits of that time.

For ten years he was the disciple of an elderly, seasoned hermit. This holy man taught him the spiritual life. St. John called him his "spiritual father." After the older monk's death, St. John spent four or five years in various monasteries. He wanted to become familiar with the way monks pray and live. Finally, John found a cave high in the rocks. The area was quiet and protected from the desert sun and winds. He divided the cave into three parts: a living room, a work room and a little chapel. People in the area brought him food and other necessities. Many also came to seek his advice about important matters. Even Emperor Theodosius I asked his advice twice, in 388 and in 392.

Such well-known saints as Augustine and Jerome wrote about the holiness of St. John. When so many people came to visit him, some men became his disciples. They stayed in the area and built a hospice. They took care of the hospice so that more people could come to benefit from the wisdom of this hermit. St. John was able to prophesy future events. He could look into the souls of those who came to him. He could read their thoughts. When he applied blessed oil on those who had a physical illness, they were often cured.

Even when John became famous, he kept humble and did not lead an easy life. He never ate before sunset. When he did eat, his food was dried fruit and vegetables. He never ate meat or cooked or warm food. St. John believed that his self-sacrificing life would help him keep close to God. He died peacefully in 394 at the age of ninety.

We can ask St. John the hermit to show us how to keep close to God. He will help us make a personal effort to let God work in and through us.

❦

MARCH 28

ST. TUTILO

Tutilo lived in the late ninth and early tenth centuries. He was educated at the Benedictine monastery of Saint-Gall. Two of his classmates have been declared "blessed." All three gradually became monks in the monastery where they had gone to school.

St. Tutilo was a person of many talents. He was a poet, a portrait painter, a sculptor, an orator and an architect. He was also a mechanic.

His greatest talent was music. He could play all the instruments known to the monks for their liturgies. He and his friend, Blessed Notker, composed tunes for the liturgy responses. Only three poems and one hymn remain of all Tutilo's works. But his paintings and sculptures are still found today in several cities of Europe. The paintings and sculptures are identified with St. Tutilo because he always marked his works with a motto.

But Tutilo was not proclaimed a saint because of his many talents. He was a humble person who wanted to live for God. He praised God the way he knew how: by painting, sculpting and composing music. Tutilo was proclaimed a saint because he spent his life praising and loving God. St. Tutilo died in 915.

Whether we have many talents or few, whether we are practical or not so practical, the important thing is to do the best we can with our lives. This is the way to show our love for God.

ST. JONAS AND ST. BARACHISIUS

King Sapor of Persia reigned in the fourth century. He hated Christians and persecuted them cruelly. He destroyed their churches and monasteries. Two brothers named Jonas and Barachisius heard of the persecutions. They learned that many Christians had been put to death.

They decided to go to help them and to encourage them to remain faithful to Christ. Jonas and Barachisius knew that they, too, might be captured. But that did not stop them. Their hearts were too full of love of others to have room for a thought of themselves.

At last the two brothers were taken prisoner. They were told that if they did not worship the sun, the moon, the fire and water, they would be tortured and put to death. Of course, they refused to worship anything or anyone except the one true God. They had to suffer greatly, but they prayed. They kept thinking of how Our Lord had suffered for them. The two brothers endured terrible tortures but would not give up their faith. They were finally condemned to death and joyfully gave up their lives for Jesus.

Jonas and Barachisius were martyred in 327.

When we have some little pain, we can ask these martyrs to help us offer it to Jesus. They will show us how to be brave and cheerful.

MARCH 30

ST. JOHN CLIMACUS

It is believed that St. John was born in Palestine in the seventh century. He seems to have been a disciple of St. Gregory Nazianzen. He could have become a famous teacher, but he decided to serve God with his whole heart. He joined a monastery on Mount Sinai when he was sixteen. Then he went to live for forty years by himself. He spent all his time praying and reading the lives of the saints.

At first, St. John was tempted by the devil. He felt all kinds of bad passions trying to make him give in and sin. But he put all his trust in Jesus and prayed harder than ever. So the temptations never made him fall into sin. In fact, he only grew holier. He became so close to God that many heard of his holiness. They came to ask him for advice.

God gave St. John a wonderful gift. He was able to bring peace to people who were upset and tempted. Once a man came to him who was having terrible temptations. He asked St. John to help him and said how hard it was for him to fight these temptations. After they had prayed together, peace filled the poor man's soul. He was never again troubled with those temptations.

When the saint was seventy-four years old, he was chosen abbot of Mount Sinai. He became the superior of all the monks and hermits in the country. Another abbot asked St. John to write the rules which he had lived by all his life. This way the monks could follow his example. With great humility, St. John wrote the book called *The Ladder of Perfection*, or *The Climax of Perfection*. And that is why he is called "Climacus." St. John died in 649.

It is very wise to keep a good book handy in our room. We can read from it a little bit each day or before we go to bed.

MARCH 31

BLESSED JOAN OF TOULOUSE

In 1240, some Carmelite brothers from Palestine started a monastery in Toulouse, France. The great Carmelite priest, St. Simon Stock, passed through Toulouse twenty-five years later. A devout woman asked to see him. She introduced herself simply as Joan. She asked the priest earnestly, "May I be part of the Carmelite order as an associate?" St. Simon Stock was the head of the order. He had the authority to grant the woman's request. He said "yes." Joan became the first lay associate. She received the habit of the Carmelite order. In the presence of St. Simon Stock, Joan made a vow of perpetual chastity.

Joan continued her quiet, simple life right in her own home. She tried to be as faithful as possible to the rules of the Carmelites for the rest of her life. Joan went to daily Mass and devotions at the Carmelite church. She filled the rest of the day with visits to the poor, the sick and the lonely. She trained the altar boys. She helped the elderly and infirm by performing useful tasks and running errands. Joan prayed with them and brightened many lives with her cheerful conversations.

Blessed Joan carried a picture of the crucified Jesus in her pocket. That was her "book." Every now and then, she would pull out the picture and gaze at it. Her eyes would light up. People said that Joan read some new and wonderful lesson every time she studied the picture.

When Blessed Joan died, she was buried in the local Carmelite church. She had been so much a part of the parish family during her lifetime.

We can ask Blessed Joan to show us how to spread the love of Jesus in our parish and neighborhood.

april

ST. HUGH OF GRENOBLE

St. Hugh was born in 1052 in France. He grew up to be tall and handsome, gentle and courteous. Although he always wanted to live for God as a monk, he was given important positions instead. He was ordained a priest and then a bishop.

As bishop, Hugh began at once to correct the sinful customs of some people in his diocese. He made wise plans, but that was not all he did. To draw God's mercy upon his people, St. Hugh prayed with his whole heart. He practiced hard penances. In a short time, many became very virtuous and pious. Only some of the nobility continued to oppose him.

Bishop Hugh still thought about the life of a monk. That's what he truly wanted. He resigned as bishop of Grenoble and entered a monastery. At last, he was at peace. Yet it was not God's will for Hugh to be a monk. After a year, the pope commanded him to go back to Grenoble again. St. Hugh obeyed. He knew it was more important to please God than to please himself.

For forty years, the bishop was sick nearly all the time. He had severe headaches and stomach problems. Yet he forced himself to keep working. He loved his people and there was so much to do for them. He suffered from trials and temptations, too. But he prayed and never gave in to sin.

St. Hugh died on April 1, 1132, two months before his eightieth birthday. He had been a generous and saintly bishop for fifty-two years. In 1134, just two years after his death, Hugh was proclaimed a saint by Pope Innocent II.

Sometimes we think we know what is best for us. Sometimes we feel more comfortable doing one thing rather than another. But if God lets us know what he has in mind, we will be glad if we follow his will. We can ask St. Hugh to help us.

APRIL 2

ST. FRANCIS OF PAOLA

St. Francis was born in the tiny village of Paola, Italy, around 1416. His parents were poor but humble and holy. They had prayed to St. Francis of Assisi for a son. When he was born, they named him after the saint. The boy went to a school taught by the Franciscan priests. There he learned to read. When he was fifteen, with his parents' permission, he went to live in a cave. He wanted to be a hermit and spend his life for God alone.

When he was twenty, other young men joined him. St. Francis left his cave. The people of Paola built a church and monastery for him and his followers. He called his new religious order the

"Minims." "Minims" means "the least of all."

Everyone loved St. Francis. He prayed for them and worked many miracles. He told his followers that they must be kind and humble, and do much penance. He himself was the best example of the virtues he preached. Once someone visited the saint and insulted him to his face. When the man was finished, Francis did something unusual. He quietly picked up some hot coals from the fireplace and closed his hands tightly around them. But he was not burned at all. "Come, warm yourself," he said to his accuser kindly. "You are shivering because you need a little charity." At such a miracle, the visitor changed his mind about Francis. From then on, he admired him greatly.

King Louis XI of France had not lived a very good life. He called for St. Francis when he was dying. Just the thought of dying made the king terrified. He wanted Francis to work a miracle to cure him. Instead, the saint gently helped the frightened man to prepare well to die a holy death. The king had a change of heart. He accepted God's will and died quietly in the arms of the saint.

St. Francis lived a long life praising and loving God. He died on Good Friday in 1507, at the age of ninety-one.

Sometimes we can get so wrapped up in loud music, television shows, videos, and computer games that we can find ourselves just living for now. We might not even give any thought or time for our souls that will live on in eternity. What should we add to our schedule that will help us reach eternal happiness with God? Daily Mass? Morning prayer? Evening prayer? Household chores done well and cheerfully? Homework done well? What else?

ST. RICHARD OF CHICHESTER

St. Richard was born in England in 1197. He and his brother became orphans when Richard was very young. His brother owned some farms. Richard gave up his studies to help him save the farms from going to ruin. He worked so hard that his grateful brother wanted to give the farms to him, but Richard would not accept them. He also chose not to marry because he wanted to go away to college to get a good education. He knew that because he had very little money, he would have to work hard to pay his tuition and support.

Richard went to Oxford University and eventually was given an important position at the university. Later, St. Edmund, who was archbishop of Canterbury, gave him responsible assignments in his diocese. When St. Edmund died, St. Richard attended the Dominican House of Studies in France. There he was ordained a priest. Then he was made the bishop of Chichester, England, and that is why he is called Richard of Chichester. King Henry III wanted someone else to be bishop. He had a friend in mind, but this person did not have the qualifications. Richard was the true bishop of Chichester. King Henry III refused to let Richard in his own cathedral. The king also threatened the people of Chichester with punishment if they offered Richard hospitality. But some brave people helped him anyway, like one of the priests of Chichester, Father Simon of Tarring. The two men became great friends. When the pope threatened to excommunicate the king, he stopped interfering and let the new bishop alone.

As bishop, St. Richard did his duties well. He was always gentle and kind with the people. Once in a while, he had to be stern. He was courageous and confronted people when they were doing wrong and were not sorry.

It is said that when St. Richard became ill, he foretold his death, because God had let him know the exact place and time when he would die. His friends, including Father Simon of Tarring, were at his bedside. He died at the age of fifty-five in 1253. He was proclaimed a saint by Pope Urban IV in 1262.

As a farmer, as a student, as a priest and bishop, St. Richard did everything well. We can ask St. Richard to help us always try our very best at home and at school.

APRIL 4

ST. ISIDORE OF SEVILLE

This saint was born in 556. Isidore's two older brothers, Leander and Fulgentius, became bishops and saints, too. Their sister, Florentina, a nun, is also a saint.

Isidore's family was probably Roman in roots. Isidore was to become the bishop of Seville, Spain. This is where he made a great impact on the Church of his day. He was bishop of Seville for thirty-seven years. During that time, he took up the work of the former bishop, his brother, St. Leander. These two brothers were responsible for the conversion of the Visigoths to the Catholic Church.

As a child, Isidore had received a first-rate education. His older brothers saw to that. He was supervised by Leander. Little Isidore thought Leander was just about the meanest person in the whole world. All he did was push the boy to do his lessons. But the day came when Isidore realized that Leander had really been a wonderful friend. He taught Isidore that we can do so much good for Jesus' Church when we take our education seriously. Isidore lived long before the Council of Trent, which started seminaries to train priests. But St. Isidore believed that every diocese should have a seminary and a Catholic school for advanced learning. Both of his dreams would some day come true when the great Catholic universities as well as seminaries would be started.

St. Isidore was an organizer, too. He was asked to direct two important Church meetings called Councils. The first was in Seville, Spain, in 619, and the other in Toledo, Spain, in 633. These Councils helped the Church be more united. This saint wrote many books, too. He wrote a history of the Goths. He wrote about Bible heroes and heroines. He even wrote a dictionary.

Bishop Isidore was available for his people. The poor of Seville knew where to go for help. There was a continuous line every day, all day, at the bishop's house. Isidore prayed and led a life of sacrifice, too. He really was a holy and much loved bishop. He died in 636. St. Isidore was proclaimed a Doctor of the Church by Pope Innocent XIII in 1722.

St. Isidore reminds us that God has given each of us a mind. It is a gift that we want to use with diligence. We can ask St. Isidore to help us apply our minds to what is worthwhile.

ST. VINCENT FERRER

A most wonderful Christian hero was St. Vincent Ferrer. He was born in Valencia, Spain, in 1350. He had a special devotion to the Blessed Mother. Whenever anyone spoke of her, it made him very happy. When he was seventeen, Vincent entered the Dominican order. He was very intelligent and did well in his studies. He was handsome too, but he wasn't proud or boastful.

First, Father Vincent taught at different colleges. Then he became a well-known preacher. The Dominicans are called the Order of Preachers. For twenty years, Father Vincent preached all over Spain and France. Although there were no microphones in those days, his voice could be heard from a great distance. Many people were converted just by listening to him. Even a well-known rabbi, Paul of Burgos, became a Catholic. He then became a priest and eventually bishop of Cartagena, Spain.

Many Catholics were so impressed by Vincent's sermons and example of holiness that they became more fervent. Catholics who were not practicing their faith often changed. They became fervent for the rest of their lives.

St. Vincent counted on God. He also asked for the prayers and penance of many people for the success of his sermons. He knew it was not his words or his talents that won people over. That is why he prayed before every sermon. But it is said that one time, when he knew that a very important person was going to listen to him, he worked harder than usual on his sermon. He ran out of time to pray. This sermon which he had prepared so carefully did not affect the nobleman much at all. God let that happen to teach Vincent not to count on himself. Another time, this same important person came to listen to Father Vincent preach. But this time the priest did not know it. He prayed and counted on God, as usual. The nobleman listened to the sermon and was greatly impressed by what he heard. When Vincent was told, he said: "In the first sermon it was Vincent who preached. In the second sermon, it was Jesus Christ."

St. Vincent died in 1419. He was proclaimed a saint by Pope Nicholas V in 1455.

Let us never brag about our good marks or any other success that comes our way. God will keep helping us all our lives if we trust him. We can ask St. Vincent to help us understand this.

BLESSED NOTKER

This Benedictine monk had once been a sickly child. He had a very noticeable speech impediment all his life. Notker was determined not to let it get in his way. This made him even more likable than he already was.

He and two other friends, Tutilo and Radpert, were very happy monks. They encouraged each other in their vocations at the monastery of Saint-Gall in Germany. Their common love for God and for music made them lifelong friends. You can read about St. Tutilo on March 28.

King Charles visited the great monastery from time to time. He highly respected Notker and asked him for advice. Unfortunately, he didn't usually follow the advice. One time King Charles sent his messenger to ask to see the monk. Notker was taking care of his garden. He sent this message: "Take care of your garden as I am taking care of mine." King Charles understood that he should be taking better care of his own soul and of his kingdom.

The king's personal chaplain was educated but very conceited. He was upset because the king valued Notker's opinion so much. In front of everybody at court one day, he asked Notker, "Since you are so intelligent, tell me what God is doing right now." The priest smiled at the monk, thinking he would never have an answer. Instead, Notker responded quickly, "God is doing now what he has always done. He is pushing down those who are proud and is raising up the lowly." The people started laughing as the chaplain quickly left the room.

Blessed Notker spent the rest of his life in his chosen vocation. He did many little extra things to make monastery life pleasant for the monks. With his friends, Tutilo and Radpert, he created beautiful music for the worship of God.

When Blessed Notker died in 912, the entire community of monks wept.

Each of us has gifts and talents. It doesn't make sense to be jealous of what someone else has received from God. We can ask Blessed Notker to help us be satisfied with the gifts we have been given.

❧

APRIL 7

ST. JOHN BAPTIST DE LA SALLE

St. John Baptist de la Salle was born in Rheims, France, on April 30, 1651. His parents were from the nobility. John was used to elegant living. But he was a devout boy, too. He loved Jesus and his Church. In fact, he was studying to become a priest when both his parents died. He had to leave the seminary and go home to take care of his brothers.

But while he was teaching and training them, he kept on studying too. His brothers turned out to be fine young men. When their studies were completed, John Baptist was ordained a priest.

At that time, the nobles, like Father de la Salle's family, had the chance to be well-educated. However, the common people remained poor and ignorant. They had no opportunity to go to school. St. John Baptist felt very sorry for the children of the poor. He decided to do something about the situation. He began to open schools for them. To provide teachers, he started a new order, the Brothers of the Christian Schools. Although Father de la Salle also taught the children himself, he spent most of his time training the teaching brothers. For them he wrote a rule of life and a book explaining the best way to teach. He was one of the best educators of all time. He believed in teaching in the language of the people, not in Latin, as others did. He grouped the students into classes. He stressed the importance of silence while the lesson was being taught.

After a while, the brothers opened more schools. They taught the sons of the working people and nobles, too. Many difficulties faced the new order. St. John Baptist's constant prayer and sacrifices blessed the work. It continued to grow and spread. Father de la Salle's health was never good. His asthma and arthritis caused him constant pain. Despite this, he would never allow himself to take on an easier lifestyle. He died on Good Friday, April 7, 1719, at the age of sixty-eight. He was proclaimed a saint by Pope Leo XIII in 1900. Pope Pius XII declared him the patron of teachers in 1950.

St. John Baptist de la Salle and his religious congregation teach us the value of an education. Do we take advantage of our opportunities to acquire an education? Apply ourselves in class? Do our homework? When we don't feel like studying, we can whisper a prayer for help to St. John Baptist de la Salle.

❧

ST. JULIE BILLIART

Mary Rose Julie Billiart was born in Belgium in 1751. Her uncle, the village school teacher, taught her to read and write. She especially loved to study her catechism. In fact, when she was just seven, Julie would explain the faith to other little children. When her parents became poor, she worked hard to help support the family. She even went to harvest the crops. Yet she always found time to pray, to visit the sick, and to teach catechism.

While she was still a young woman, she became very ill and completely paralyzed. Although helpless, St. Julie offered her prayers so that many people would find eternal happiness with God. She was more united to God than ever and kept on teaching catechism from bed. She was a very spiritual person. People came to her for advice because she helped them grow closer to Jesus and practice their faith with more love. She encouraged all to receive Holy Communion often. Many young women were inspired by Julie's love for God. They were willing to spend their time and money for good works. With Julie as their leader, they started the Sisters of Notre Dame de Namur.

Once a priest gave a mission in the town where Julie was. He asked her to make a novena with him for an intention which he would not tell her. After five days, on the feast of the Sacred Heart, he said: "Mother, if you have faith, take one step in honor of the Sacred Heart of Jesus." Mother Billiart, who had been paralyzed for twenty-two years, stood up and was cured!

St. Julie spent the rest of her life training young women to become sisters. She watched over her congregation. She had to suffer much from those who did not understand her mission, but she always trusted God. Her favorite words were: "How good is the good God." He assured her that someday her religious congregation would be very large. And that is just what happened. Although St. Julie died on April 8, 1816, today there are many of St. Julie's sisters all over the world. Mother Julie was proclaimed a saint by Pope Paul VI in 1969.

When something is worrying us, such as a test in school or troubles at home, let us often say: "Sacred Heart of Jesus, I trust in you."

APRIL 9

ST. WALDETRUDIS

Waldetrudis was born in Belgium in the seventh century. Her mother, her father and her sister have all been declared saints. She grew up to be a beautiful girl. Even when she was enjoying herself, she had a way of edifying people. Several young men wanted to marry her. In those days, parents chose husbands for their daughters. Her parents chose Count Madelgar. They could not have picked a better man, because he became a saint too. He is St. Vincent Madelgar. The couple had four children. Incredibly, all have been declared saints.

St. Waldetrudis was happy that God had given her such a wonderful family. Yet she had to suffer very much in her lifetime. Jealous ladies spread terrible stories about her. The women were not pure and kind as she was. They did not want people to think that she was better than they. So they said she only prayed and did good deeds to hide her secret sins. Of course, that was a lie, but the saint did not defend herself. She thought of how Jesus had suffered on the cross and, like him, she forgave her enemies.

Quite a while after the birth of their last child, St. Vincent explained that he wanted very much to be a monk. In fact, he hoped to spend the rest of his life in the monastery. His wife understood and gave him her permission. St. Vincent made sure that his family was well-provided for. The couple was going to miss each other very much. But Waldetrudis would not hold her husband back. She made the sacrifice for God.

Two years later, Waldetrudis decided to become a nun. She lived a very self-sacrificing life and was generous with the poor. People came to her for spiritual advice and some who came reported healings. St. Waldetrudis died in 688. After her death, many people who prayed at her tomb reported miraculous healings.

This saint helps us realize that there are many good things in our lives. We should thank God for them. But there are also sad things at times. We should pray to have the courage to act as Jesus would in those situations.

APRIL 10

BLESSED ANTHONY NEYROT

Anthony was born in northern Italy in the fifteenth century. He joined the Dominican order in Florence, Italy. The prior at that time was another saint, Antoninus. We celebrate his feast on May 10. This saint was to have a great influence on Blessed Anthony.

Brother Anthony was sailing from Naples to Sicily when pirates captured the ship. Anthony was taken to Tunis and sold as a slave. He was able to win his freedom, but fell away from the Church. He denied his faith in Jesus and abandoned his religious vocation. He accepted the Koran, the sacred book of the Muslims. For several months, he practiced the Muslim religion. He also married.

In the meantime, his former Dominican prior, the saintly Antoninus, died. This led Anthony to have a shocking experience. It seems that one night, Anthony had something like a dream. St. Antoninus appeared to him. The conversation between the two men was to lead to a radical change in Anthony. He became truly sorry for having betrayed the Lord. He knew that in his heart he could never give up his faith in Jesus. He knew that he could only be a Catholic. And he realized that he still wanted very much to be a Dominican brother.

Blessed Anthony sent his wife back to her family. He then put on his white Dominican habit. In spite of his fear, he went to see the ruler of Tunis. A large crowd gathered and the ruler came out to the courtyard. Brother Anthony publicly admitted he had made a terrible mistake. He was a Catholic. He believed in and loved Jesus. He was a Dominican and wanted to be so for all his life. The ruler was angry. He threatened and then made promises of rewards if only Anthony would take back what he was saying. But Anthony would not. He knew this meant his death.

Anthony knelt and began to pray for the courage to give his life for Jesus. Suddenly he felt the large stones pounding him. He just kept praying for the strength to remain true to the Lord. Then he lost consciousness. Anthony died a martyr in 1460. Some merchants from Genoa, Italy, took his remains back to his own country.

Blessed Anthony gives us courage. Jesus will always forgive us our mistakes and sins when we are sorry.

❧❦

APRIL 11

ST. STANISLAUS

St. Stanislaus was born near Cracow, Poland, in 1030. His parents had prayed for thirty years for a child. When Stanislaus was born, they offered him to God because they were so grateful to have him. When he grew up, he studied in Paris, France. After his parents died, he gave all the money and property they had left him to the poor. Then he became a priest.

In 1072, Stanislaus was made the bishop of Cracow. (Before he became pope, John Paul II was also bishop of Cracow many centuries later.) Bishop Stanislaus won the love of all the people. They especially appreciated the way he took care of the poor, the widows and the orphans. Often he served them himself.

Poland's king at that time was Boleslaus II. He was cruel and impure. The people were disgusted with his lifestyle and were afraid of him. Bishop Stanislaus first corrected him privately. The bishop was kind and respectful. But he was honest, too, about what the king was doing wrong. The king seemed sorry, but soon fell back into his old ways again. He committed even more shameful sins. The bishop then had to put him out of the Church. King Boleslaus flew into a rage at that. To get revenge, he ordered two of his guards to kill St. Stanislaus. Three times they tried and failed. Then the king himself, in a mad rage, rushed into the bishop's chapel. He murdered St. Stanislaus as he was celebrating Mass. It was April 11, 1079.

God worked many miracles after St. Stanislaus' death. All the people called him a martyr. He was proclaimed a saint by Pope Innocent IV in 1253.

We admire and appreciate St. Stanislaus. It takes courage to correct people who are hurting others and giving a bad example. Sometimes we might have to be corrected for our own mistakes. Let us ask St. Stanislaus to help us correct our faults and bad habits. Let us ask him also to be grateful to those who challenge us to become better.

ST. JOSEPH MOSCATI

Joseph Moscati was born on July 25, 1880, in Benevento, Italy. He was the seventh of nine children. His father became a judge in Naples, so the entire family moved there. When Joseph was twelve, his older brother Albert was thrown from a horse. The family hoped for a cure at first, but the boy's condition worsened. Joseph spent much of his free time at his brother's bedside. He was there when Albert died.

His brother's death made a deep impression on Joseph. He asked Jesus in the Eucharist and Mary for answers. Suffering had to have a purpose. He also became convinced of the importance of expert medical care. Most important though, he realized that in this life we are journeying toward eternity. It is up to us to help people and serve them as we journey. Joseph wondered and prayed about what he should do with his life. He decided that he wanted to help cure physical pain. Joseph would become a doctor.

When he was twenty-three, Dr. Moscati began his service at the Hospital of the Incurables in Naples. Later he opened his own office. All patients were welcome whether they could pay or not. He would write prescriptions for poor patients, then pay for the medicine out of his own pocket. Every day was long and hard, but Dr.

Moscati remained gentle and kind. He made the effort to listen carefully to his patients. He encouraged them and prayed for them.

Besides being an excellent doctor, he was holy too. How did he do it? Each morning he went to Mass and spent time in prayer. Then the doctor would visit the sick poor in the slums of Naples. From there he would go to the hospital and begin his rounds. For twenty-four years, Joseph worked and prayed for his patients. He poured all his strength into his life's calling. On the afternoon of April 12, 1927, Dr. Moscati did not feel well, so he went to his office and relaxed in an arm chair. There he had a stroke and died. He was forty-seven.

Dr. Joseph Moscati was proclaimed a saint by Pope John Paul II on October 25, 1987.

We can ask St. Joseph Moscati to help us be honest, kind and sympathetic as he was. We can also ask him to teach us how to appreciate the Mass and to love Mary as he did.

APRIL 13

ST. MARTIN I

St. Martin was a priest of Rome who had a reputation for being well-educated and holy. He became pope in July, 649. When people were arguing over the truths about Jesus, Pope Martin called a meeting of bishops. This meeting was the Council of the Lateran. It explained clearly what we believe about certain truths. However, some Christians were not pleased about it. Pope Martin knew the Council's explanations were true. It was his duty as pope to teach people the truth.

Some powerful men did not appreciate Pope Martin's activities. One such person was Emperor Constans II of Constantinople. He sent his soldiers to Rome to capture Martin and bring him to Constantinople. The soldiers kidnapped the pope. They took him right out of the Lateran Cathedral and snuck him onto a ship. Pope Martin got sick, but they continued their journey. In October, 653, he was put in jail in Constantinople for three months. He was given only a little food and water each day. He wasn't even allowed to wash himself. Pope Martin was put on trial, publicly humiliated and condemned to death. But then he was sent back to the same prison for three more months. Patriarch Paul of Constantinople pleaded for the pope's life. So instead of death, the pope was sentenced to be exiled. Pope Martin was put on a ship that took him across the Black Sea. In April, 654, it landed on the Russian peninsula called the Crimea.

Pope Martin was shocked at the neglect he suffered from those who were in charge of his captivity. He wrote his own account of those sad days. The pope said that he felt very bad to be forgotten by his relatives and members of the Church in Rome. He knew they were afraid of the emperor. But at least, he said, they could have sent supplies of corn, oil and other basic needs. But they did not. They abandoned the pope because of fear.

The pope's exile lasted two years. He died around 656. Because of his terrible sufferings, he was proclaimed a martyr. He is the last of the popes so far to be considered a martyr.

Sometimes we might fall into the trap of envying people in powerful positions. It is then that we should pray to St. Martin I. We can ask him to replace our ambition with the kind of courage he had.

APRIL 14

BLESSED LIDWINA

The name Lidwina means "suffering." Lidwina was from Holland. She was born in 1380 and died in 1433. When she was fifteen, Lidwina dedicated herself completely to God. She might have eventually become a nun. But in a single afternoon, her entire life was changed.

The girl went skating with her friends. One of them accidentally bumped her. Lidwina fell down hard on the ice and broke a rib. She was in pain. But the fall triggered other problems, too. In the days ahead, she had severe headaches, nausea, fever, pain throughout her whole body and thirst.

Crying, Lidwina told her father she could not stand the pain anymore. But the pain increased. She developed sores on her face and body. She became blind in one eye. Finally, she could no longer leave her bed.

Lidwina was frustrated and bitter. Why had God let this happen to her? What did he want from her? And what could she still give to him anyway? Her parish priest, Father John, came to visit and pray with her. He helped her think of what Jesus had suffered. She began to realize the beautiful gift that she would give to Jesus: she would suffer for him. She would offer her sufferings to console him, who had suffered so much on the cross. Her suffering became a beautiful prayer to God. Little by little, Lidwina began to understand.

For thirty-eight years, Lidwina suffered. It seemed impossible that she could remain alive in such serious condition. But she did. God comforted her in many ways. Lidwina was good to everyone who came to her poor little room. She prayed to God and suffered for their special intentions. They knew God would listen to Lidwina.

Lidwina's special love was for Jesus in the Holy Eucharist. For many years, she seemed to live only on Holy Communion.

Blessed Lidwina helps us see that we can offer physical pain to Jesus with love. She reminds us, too, that if we have good health, we should thank God often.

BLESSED DAMIEN OF MOLOKAI

Joseph "Jeff" de Veuster was born in 1840, the son of Belgian farmers. He and his brother, Pamphile, joined the congregation of the Sacred Hearts. These missionaries were responsible for the Catholic faith on the Hawaiian Islands. Jeff chose the name "Damien." Brother Damien was tall and strong. His years of helping on the family farm had given him a healthy look. Everybody liked him because he was good-natured and generous.

More missionaries were needed in the kingdom of Hawaii. In 1863, a group of Sacred Hearts priests and brothers were chosen to go. Pamphile, Damien's brother, was selected. Just before the departure date, Pamphile came down with typhoid fever. He could no longer consider going to the missions. Brother Damien, still studying to become a priest, asked to take his place. The father general accepted Damien's offer. He went home to his family for a loving farewell. Then he took the ship from Belgium to Hawaii, a journey of eighteen weeks. Damien finished his studies and was ordained a priest in Hawaii. He spent eight years among the people of three districts. He traveled on horseback and by canoe.

The people loved this tall, generous priest. He saw that they responded to ceremonies. He used the little money he could raise to build chapels. He

and volunteer parishioners built the chapels themselves. But the most incredible part of Damien's life was soon to begin. The bishop asked for a volunteer priest to go to the island of Molokai. The very name struck the people with fear and dread. They knew that the section of the island called *Kalawao* was the "living graveyard" of people dying of leprosy. There was so much ignorance about the disease and such great fear of contagion that lepers were mostly abandoned. Many just despaired. There was no priest, no law enforcement agent on Molokai, no health-care facilities. The Hawaiian government sent some food and medical supplies, but it was not sufficient. And there were no organized means to distribute the goods.

Father Damien went to Molokai. Faced with the poverty, corruption and despair, even Damien was shaken. But he made up his mind that for him there was no turning back. The people were desperately in need of help. He went to Honolulu to confront the members of the board of health. They told him that he could not travel back and forth to Molokai for fear of contagion. Their real reason was that they didn't want him on Molokai. He was creating too many problems for them. So Damien had to make a choice: if he went back to Molokai, he could never leave. The board of health didn't know Damien. He chose Molokai.

He labored for eighteen years until his death on Molokai. With the help of the lepers and generous volunteers, Molokai was transformed. The word *Molokai* took on a whole different meaning. It became an island of Christian love. Father Damien eventually became a leper himself. He died on April 15, 1889, at the age of forty-nine and was buried there. He was proclaimed "blessed" by Pope John Paul II in 1994.

We can ask Blessed Damien to give us some of his courage and generosity. There are so many people who need our love and support. Blessed Damien will help us respond with his joy and good-heartedness.

❧

APRIL 16

ST. BENEDICT JOSEPH LABRE

This French saint, born in 1748, led a most unusual life. He was the son of a store owner and was taught by his uncle, a priest. When the good priest died, Benedict tried to enter a monastery. However, he was told he was too young. Then he contacted another order of monks. He loved the life of prayer and penance. But when he joined them, Benedict became thin and frail. It was suggested that he return home to lead a good Christian life. He went home and slowly gained back his health. He prayed for God's help. Then he felt he was given an answer. He would become a pilgrim, a person on a holy journey of prayer and penance. As a pilgrim, he would travel to the famous shrines of Europe.

Benedict began his journey on foot. He visited one church after another. He wore a plain cloth robe, a crucifix over his heart and a rosary around his neck. He slept on the bare ground. The only food he had was what kind people gave him. If they gave him money, he passed it on to the poor. His "suitcase" was a sack. In it he carried his own Gospel, as well as medals and holy books to give to others. St. Benedict paid no attention to the beautiful sights in the cities he visited. His only interest was in the churches where Jesus dwelt in the Blessed Sacrament.

As the years passed, St. Benedict looked more and more like a beggar. He was ragged and dirty. He ate crusts of bread and potato peels. He never asked for anything that would make his life more comfortable. In some places, children threw stones at him and called him names. People who didn't know him tended to avoid him. But when St. Benedict knelt in front of the tabernacle, he became as still as a statue. His pale, tired face glowed. He would talk to Jesus and to the Blessed Mother. He would whisper, "Mary, O my Mother!" He was truly happy when he was keeping Jesus and the Blessed Mother company.

He died in 1783 at the age of thirty-five. The fame of this poor holy man spread far and wide. His journey had ended. The pilgrimage was over and he would be with Jesus and Mary forever. A century after his death, St. Benedict Joseph Labre was proclaimed a saint by Pope Leo XIII in 1883.

We cannot imitate the poverty of Jesus in the way St. Benedict Joseph did. We can imitate this saint's love for the Blessed Sacrament, however. Let us go to church often to visit and to have a heart-to-heart talk with him. Jesus is our best friend, too.

ST. STEPHEN HARDING

Stephen was a young Englishman who lived in the twelfth century. He was a good student who liked to learn. Stephen was especially interested in literature. He was serious about life and prayed daily. Once Stephen and his friend set out on foot as pilgrims for Rome. When they returned, Stephen joined a very poor and holy group of monks. These men prayed, fasted and worked hard. That was their way of showing their love for God. Stephen noticed how happy they were. Their abbot was another saint, St. Robert.

For a while, Stephen served God joyfully with them. But little by little the monks did not want to live such a strict life anymore. So St. Robert and St. Stephen and twenty of the monks started a new monastery. They built it themselves in the wilderness in France called Citeaux. They lived a life of work and great poverty. They wanted to imitate the poverty of Jesus. They kept strict silence.

When St. Stephen became the abbot, he had many troubles. The monks had just a little food. Then over half of the monks became sick and died. It looked as though the community would come to an end. They needed new, young members to continue their life. Stephen prayed with faith. And his prayer was rewarded. God sent to these monks called Cistercians thirty young men who wanted to join them. They arrived at the monastery gate all together. Their leader was to become a great saint, too. His name is St. Bernard. We celebrate his feast day on August 20. This was a marvelous day for St. Stephen and the monks.

St. Stephen spent the last few years of his life writing a book of rules for the monks. He also trained St. Bernard to take his place.

When he lay dying, St. Stephen heard the monks around him whispering. They were saying that Stephen did not have to be afraid to die. He had worked so hard and loved God so much. But St. Stephen said that he was afraid he had not been good enough. And he really meant it. That shows us how humble this great saint was. He died in 1134.

We often live in noise all day, all evening. We listen to the radio, watch TV, and play computer and video games. Our heads are filled with sounds. We can ask St. Stephen the monk to help us to find some "quiet time" each day. That's when we'll let God work in our minds and hearts. But we have to pray to be wise enough to take the time.

BLESSED MARY
OF THE INCARNATION

Barbara was born in France in 1566. She was married to Peter Acarie when she was seventeen. She and her husband loved their Catholic faith and practiced it. The couple had six children and their family life was happy. Barbara tried to be a good wife and mother. Her family learned from her a great love for prayer and works of charity.

Once, when her husband was accused unjustly of a crime, Barbara herself saved him. She went to court, and, all alone, proved that he was not guilty.

Although she was busy with her own family, she always found time to feed those who were hungry. She instructed people in the faith. She helped the sick and dying. She gently encouraged people who were living sinfully to change their ways. The good deeds she performed were works of mercy.

When her husband died, Barbara entered the Carmelite order. She was to spend the last four years of her life as a nun. Her three daughters had become Carmelites, too. Barbara's new name as a nun was Sister Mary of the Incarnation. She joyfully worked in the kitchen among the pots and pans. When her own daughter became the superior of the monastery, Blessed Mary willingly obeyed her. So humble was she that as she was dying, she said: "The Lord forgive the bad example I have given you." The nuns were really surprised because she had tried so hard to live a good life. Blessed Mary died in 1618. She was fifty-two.

Blessed Mary became close to God even though her life was busy. She had many responsibilities. She took care of her family. She also was thoughtful about helping others. She can help us to be responsible and generous with our lives, too.

APRIL 19

BLESSED JAMES DUCKETT

James Duckett was an Englishman who lived during the reign of Queen Elizabeth I. As a young man he became an apprentice printer in London. This is how he came across a book called *The Firm Foundation of the Catholic Religion.* He studied it carefully and believed that the Catholic Church was the true Church. In those days, Catholics were persecuted in England. James decided that he wanted to be a Catholic anyway and would face the consequences. The clergyman at his former church came to look for him because James had been a steady church goer. He would not come back. Twice he served short prison terms for his stubbornness. Both times his employer interceded and got him freed. But then the employer asked

James to find a job elsewhere.

James Duckett knew there was no turning back. He sought out a disguised Catholic priest in the Gatehouse prison. The old priest, "Mr. Weekes," instructed him. Duckett was received into the Catholic Church. He married a Catholic widow and their son became a Carthusian monk. He recorded much of what we know about his father.

Blessed Duckett never forgot that it was a book that had started him on the road to the Church. He considered it his responsibility to provide his neighbors with Catholic books. He knew these books encouraged and instructed them. So dangerous was this "occupation" that he was in prison for nine out of twelve years of his married life. He was finally brought to trial and condemned to death on the testimony of one man, Peter Bullock, a book binder. He testified that he had bound Catholic books for Blessed Duckett, a "grave offense." Bullock turned traitor because he was in prison for unrelated matters and hoped to be freed.

Both men were condemned to die on the same day. On the scaffold at Tyburn, Blessed Duckett assured Bullock of his forgiveness. He kept encouraging the man as they were dying to accept the Catholic faith. Then the ropes were placed around their necks. Blessed Duckett was martyred in 1602.

If we need to be convinced of the power of media—books, television shows, radio programs, videos, cassettes—we can pray to Blessed Duckett. We can ask him to help us realize the influence that good Catholic media can have on our lives.

ST. AGNES OF MONTEPULCIANO

This saint was born near the city of Montepulciano, Italy, in 1268. When she was just nine years old, she begged her mother and father to let her live at the nearby convent. Agnes was very happy with the sisters. They led a quiet, prayerful life. They worked hard, too. Even though she was young, Agnes understood why the sisters lived and prayed so well. They wanted to be very close to Jesus.

The years passed. St. Agnes received her training as a novice. She was such a good nun that the other sisters were pleased to have her. Agnes prayed with all her heart. She gave the sisters a good example. Some young women came to join them. Agnes and the sisters belonged to the Order of Preachers, called Dominicans.

Eventually, Agnes was chosen superior or "prioress" of the convent. She tried to be fair and honest with each sister. She kept reminding herself that everything she did was for Jesus. She believed that Jesus was really in charge of the convent. He was taking care of them.

Mother Agnes performed hard penances. She was kind and gentle even when she didn't feel like it. God filled Agnes with joy and sometimes gave her spiritual favors. One time he even let her hold the Christ Child in her arms.

Agnes was a sickly woman. But she was patient even when she was very ill. She never complained or felt sorry for herself. Instead, she offered everything to God. Toward the end of her life, the sisters realized she was not going to get better. They were very sad. "If you loved me, you would be glad," Agnes said. "I am going to enter the glory of Jesus."

St. Agnes died in 1317 at the age of forty-nine. She was proclaimed a saint in 1726. Her tomb became a place of pilgrimage. Many people came to pray to this holy woman and to seek her help. Among the pilgrims was the famous St. Catherine of Siena. We celebrate St. Catherine's feast day on April 29.

From St. Agnes we can learn that the Lord has something in mind for each of us. He gives us talents and opportunities to do our best with our life's calling. We can ask the Lord often to help us become what he wants us to.

APRIL 21

ST. ANSELM

Anselm was born in northern Italy in 1033. From his home he could see the Alps mountains. When he was fifteen, Anselm tried to join a monastery in Italy. But his father was against it. Then Anselm became sick. Not long after he got better, his mother died. He was still young and rich and clever. Soon he forgot about wanting to serve God. He began to think only of having good times.

After a while though, Anselm became bored with this way of life. He wanted something better, something more important. He went to France to visit the holy Abbot Lanfranc of the famous monastery of Bec. Anselm became Lanfranc's very close friend and the abbot brought him to God. He also helped Anselm decide to become a Benedictine monk. Anselm was then twenty-seven.

Anselm was a warm-hearted man who loved his brother monks dearly. Even those who first resented him soon became his friends. He became the abbot in 1078. When he had to leave Bec to become archbishop of Canterbury in England, he told the monks that they would always live in his heart.

The people of England loved and respected Anselm. However, King William II persecuted him. Anselm had to flee into exile in 1097 and in 1103. King William even forbade Anselm to go to Rome to ask the pope's advice. But Anselm went anyway. He stayed with the pope until the king died. Then he went back to his diocese in England.

Even in the midst of his many duties, St. Anselm always found time to write important books of philosophy and theology. He also wrote down the many wonderful instructions he had given the monks about God. They were very happy about that. He used to say: "Would you like to know the secret of being happy in the monastery? Forget the world and be happy to forget it.

The monastery is a real heaven on earth for those who live only for Jesus." St. Anselm died on April 21, 1109. He was declared a great teacher or Doctor of the Church by Pope Clement XI in 1720.

There's nothing wrong with having good, clean fun. What we have to remember, though, is that all the fun in the world won't make us happy. We will only be really happy when we are spending our time doing worthwhile things for God and our neighbors.

APRIL 22

ST. SOTER AND ST. CAIUS

St. Soter was pope long ago in the times of the Roman emperors. He was a real father to all Christians. He gave much help to those who were poor. He took special care of those who had been condemned to work in dangerous mines. They were sent there because they would not give up their faith in Jesus. These brave Christians were hungry all the time. They were allowed only a little rest. Other Christians were chained in prisons. Good Pope Soter did everything he possibly could to comfort and help them.

St. Soter also helped Christians who were far away from Rome. This holy pope was a great preacher. All the Christians loved to listen to him explain our religion. He spoke with such love. He inspired them with the courage to die for Jesus rather than sacrifice to false gods. St. Soter himself gave his life for Jesus in the year 174 after having been pope for ten years.

St. Caius was pope about one hundred years later. He, too, lived in times of persecution. This pope did all he could to prepare people to keep the faith at any sacrifice. To be of more help to his people, he lived eight years in underground rooms, called catacombs. These were cemeteries where the Christians often met in secret to pray and receive the sacraments. This was their hiding place from the cruel pagan soldiers. The Christians knew they would be killed if they were caught.

St. Caius was pope for twelve years. Then he, too, was martyred. He died in the year 296.

Today people in different parts of the world are still persecuted because they are good Christians. Let us offer our prayers and sacrifices that Jesus may comfort them and give them courage.

APRIL 23

ST. GEORGE

Pictures of St. George usually show him killing a dragon to rescue a beautiful lady. The dragon stands for wickedness. The lady stands for God's holy truth. St. George is slaying the dragon because he has won the battle against the devil.

Not much is known about St. George except

that he was a martyr. He was a soldier in the army of Diocletian, a pagan emperor. Diocletian was a bitter enemy of the Christians. In fact, he put to death every Christian he could find.

It is believed that St. George was one of Diocletian's favorite soldiers. When George became a Christian, he went to the emperor and scolded him for being so cruel. Then he gave up his position in the Roman army. St. George paid a very high price for his bravery. He was cruelly tortured and beheaded.

So boldly daring and so cheerful was St. George in declaring his faith that people felt courage when they heard about it. Many songs and poems were written about this martyr. Soldiers, especially, have always been devoted to him. He was named the patron of England in 1222.

St. George was killed in Lydda, Palestine, around the year 303.

We all have some "dragon" we have to conquer. It might be selfishness or anger. It might be laziness or greed, or something else. We can ask St. George to help us fight against these "dragons." He will help us if we ask.

ST. FIDELIS OF SIGMARINGEN

This saint's name was Mark Rey. He was born in Germany in 1578. Mark went to the famous University of Freiburg to become a lawyer. Even as a student, he liked to visit the sick and the poor. He spent time praying daily. His brother chose to be a Capuchin Franciscan priest. Mark, instead, finished his studies and became a famous lawyer.

Mark often took on the cases of poor people who had no money to pay. This won him the nickname, "The Poor Man's Lawyer." Because he was very honest, Mark became disgusted with the dishonesty of the law courts. He decided to follow his brother and become a priest. He received his religious habit and took the name Fidelis, which means "faithful."

Father Fidelis was filled with joy when he was assigned to Switzerland to preach the Good News. At that time in Switzerland there were many enemies of the Catholic faith. Father Fidelis wanted to win these people back to the Church. His preaching brought wonderful results. Many people were converted. Enemies of the Church grew angry at his success.

St. Fidelis admitted that his life was in danger, yet went right on preaching. In the middle of a sermon one day, a shot was fired, but the bullet missed. Father Fidelis knew he had to leave the town at once. He did, but as he was walking down the road to the next town, a mob of angry men stopped him. They ordered the priest to give up the Catholic religion. St. Fidelis said firmly, "I will not give up the Catholic faith." The men pounced on him with their clubs and crude tools.

The wounded priest pulled himself up to a kneeling position. He prayed: "Lord, forgive my enemies. They do not know what they are doing. Lord Jesus, have mercy on me! Holy Mary, my Mother, help me!" The men attacked him again until they were certain he was dead.

St. Fidelis died a martyr in 1622 at the age of forty-four. He was proclaimed a saint by Pope Benedict XIV in 1746.

It is a great honor to be able to help others come back to Jesus, back to the Church. Let us try, by prayer, good example and kind words, to be real apostles.

APRIL 25

ST. MARK THE EVANGELIST

Mark lived at the time of Jesus. Although he was not among the original twelve apostles, he was a relative of St. Barnabas, an apostle. Mark is well-known because he wrote one of the four Gospels. That is why he is called an evangelist, a Gospel writer. Mark's Gospel is short, but it gives many little details that are not in the other Gospels.

While still young, Mark went with the two great saints, Paul and Barnabas, on a missionary journey to bring the teachings of Jesus to new lands. Before the journey was over, though, Mark seems to have had a disagreement with St. Paul. Mark suddenly returned to Jerusalem. Paul and Mark later worked out their differences. In fact, Paul wrote from prison in Rome that Mark came to console and help him.

Mark also became a beloved disciple of St. Peter, the first pope. St. Peter called St. Mark "my son." Some think that Peter meant to say that he had baptized Mark. Mark was consecrated a bishop and sent to Alexandria, Egypt. There he converted many people. He worked hard to spread love for Jesus and his Church. It is believed that he went through long and painful sufferings before he died.

St. Mark's relics were brought to Venice, Italy. He is the patron saint of that famous city. People go to the beautiful basilica of St. Mark to honor him and to pray to him.

We can remember St. Mark when we have a disagreement with someone. We can think of him also when we can't get along with people even if we want to. At those difficult moments, we can ask St. Mark to show us his secret for patching up differences.

ST. RADBERTUS

This saint lived in ninth-century France. No one knows who his parents were. They left their newborn infant on the doorstep of Notre-Dame convent. The nuns loved and cared for the baby. They named him Radbertus. When he was old enough to be educated, Radbertus was sent to the monks of St. Peter nearby.

The boy loved learning and especially enjoyed the Latin classics. When he grew up, he lived a quiet, scholarly life. He remained a lay person for several years. Then he felt the call to become a monk. He joined a community led by two fervent abbots, St. Adalhard and his brother who succeeded him, Abbot Wala. Radbertus tried to be a holy monk. He often accompanied the two abbots on their journeys. He wrote their biographies after they died.

Radbertus became a Scripture scholar. He wrote a long commentary on the Gospel of St. Matthew. He produced other explanations of parts of the Bible, too. But his most well-known work is called "The Body and Blood of Christ."

Radbertus did not feel that he had a vocation to be a priest. But he was persuaded to accept the appointment of abbot for a seven-year term. Then he insisted that he return to his life of prayer, meditation, study and writing. His term as abbot was very difficult for him although he did the best he could. He spent the rest of his life praying, writing and doing the tasks assigned him.

Radbertus died in 860.

St. Radbertus reminds us of the sacredness of every human life. He was an abandoned baby, yet look at the wonderful gifts God had given him. Let us ask him to inspire legislators to pass wise laws that protect human life in all its stages.

APRIL 27

ST. ZITA

Zita is known as the patron saint of domestic workers. She was born in the village of Monte Sagrati, Italy, in 1218. Her parents were deeply religious and raised Zita in a loving, Christian way. It was the custom of poor couples to send their teenage daughters to trustworthy families who could afford servants. The young women would live with the families for a time and were employed to do the domestic tasks. Zita was sent to the Fatinelli family in Lucca when she was twelve.

Mr. and Mrs. Fatinelli were good people who had several workers. Zita was happy to be able to work and send money to her parents. She tried to live responsibly. She formed habits of praying that fit in with her schedule. She rose early to go to daily Mass.

Zita was diligent in her work. She felt it was part of her very self. But the other workers were annoyed. They tried to do as little as they could get away with. They began to pick on Zita and oppose her without their employers noticing. Zita was hurt but she prayed for patience. She never told on the workers. She insisted on doing her work as well as possible no matter what they thought.

When one of the workers tried to kiss her, Zita fought him off. He left the room with several scratches on his face. Mr. Fatinelli questioned her privately about the incident. She told him honestly what had happened. After that, Zita became the head housekeeper. The Fatinelli children were placed under her care. Best of all, the other workers stopped persecuting her. Some even began to imitate her.

Zita spent her whole life with the Fatinelli family. While others came and went, she stayed. She served them lovingly. She loved them like she loved her own family. By her example, she helped people see that work is beautiful when it is done with Christian love. Zita died peacefully on April 27, 1278. She was sixty years old.

Zita has a wonderful lesson for us all. She reminds us that what we do is part of who we are. Our work and our study take effort. But they are worth the trouble because the Lord will reward our diligence in heaven.

ST. PETER CHANEL

St. Peter Chanel was born near Belley, France, in 1803. From the time he was seven, he took care of his father's sheep. Though poor, he was intelligent and loved his faith, too. One day, a good parish priest met him. He thought so much of Peter that he asked his parents if he could educate the boy. In this priest's little school, and later in the seminary, Peter studied hard. When he became a priest, he was sent to a parish where just a few Catholics still practiced their faith. Father Chanel was prayerful. He was kind and patient with everyone. In just three years there was a big improvement. Many people became full of love for Jesus and his Church again.

St. Peter Chanel had a great desire to become a missionary. He joined a religious order called Marist missionaries. He hoped he would be sent to bring the Gospel to people who did not yet believe in God. After a few years, his wish came true. He and a group of Marist missionaries were sent to the islands of the South Pacific. Father Chanel and one brother were assigned to the island of Futuna. There the people willingly listened to Father Chanel preach. "This man loves us," one of the people said. "And he himself practices what he teaches us to do."

Unfortunately, the chief of this tribe became

jealous of the priest's success. When the chief's own son was baptized, he was furious. He sent a band of his warriors to kill the missionary. All the priest said as he lay dying was, "It is well with me." St. Peter Chanel was killed on April 28, 1841. Within a short time after his martyrdom, the whole island became Christian. Peter was declared a saint by Pope Pius XII in 1954.

Jealousy leads people to do many evil things. If we see others doing good, let us thank God for it. We can also try to imitate their good example.

APRIL 29

ST. CATHERINE OF SIENA

Born in 1347, this well-known saint is the patroness of Italy, her country. Catherine was the youngest in a family of twenty-five children. Her mother and father wanted her to be happily married. However, Catherine wished only to be a nun. To prove her point, she cut off her long, beautiful hair. She wanted to make herself unattractive. Her parents were very upset and scolded her frequently. They also gave her the heaviest housework to do. But Catherine did not back down. Finally, her parents stopped opposing her.

St. Catherine was very honest and straightforward with Jesus. Once she asked him, "Where were you, Lord, when I had such shameful temptations?" And Jesus answered, "Daughter, I was in your heart. I made you win with my grace." One night, many people of Siena were out on the streets celebrating. Jesus appeared to Catherine who was praying alone in her room. With Jesus was his Blessed Mother. She took Catherine's hand and lifted it up to her Son. Jesus put a ring on the saint's finger and she became his bride.

In Catherine's time, the Church had many problems. There were fights going on all over Italy. Catherine wrote letters to kings and queens. She even went to beg rulers to make peace with the pope and to avoid wars. Catherine asked the pope to leave Avignon, France, and return to Rome to rule the Church. She told him it was God's will. He listened to St. Catherine and did what she said.

Catherine never forgot that Jesus was in her heart. Through her, Jesus helped the sick people she nursed. Through her Jesus comforted the prisoners she visited in jail.

This great saint died in Rome in 1380. She was just thirty-three. She was proclaimed a saint by Pope Pius II in 1461. In 1970, Pope Paul VI declared St. Catherine a Doctor of the Church. She received this great honor because she served Jesus' Church heroically during her brief lifetime.

Let us offer our whole hearts to God. Then, like St. Catherine, we will discover how wonderful it is to love the Lord.

APRIL 30

ST. PIUS V

This holy pope was born in Italy in 1504. He was baptized Anthony Ghislieri. He wanted to become a priest, but it seemed as though his dream would never come true. His parents were poor. They had no money to send him to school. One day, two Dominicans came to his home and met Anthony. They liked him so much that they offered to educate him. And so at the age of fourteen, Anthony joined the Dominican order. That is when he took the name "Michael." Eventually, he became a priest. Then he became a bishop and cardinal.

Courageously he defended the teachings of the Church against those who opposed them. He continued to live a life of penance. When he was sixty-one, he was chosen pope. He took the name Pope Pius V. He had once been a poor shepherd boy. Now he was the head of the whole Catholic Church. Yet he remained as humble as ever. He still wore his white Dominican habit, the same old one he had always worn. And no one could persuade him to change it.

As pope, Pius V had many challenges to face. He drew strength from the crucifix. He meditated every day on the sufferings and death of Jesus. At this time, the Turks were trying to conquer the whole Christian world. They had a great navy on the Mediterranean Sea. A Christian force went to battle them at a place called Lepanto, near Greece. From the moment the army set out, the pope prayed the Rosary. He encouraged the people to do the same. Thanks to the help of the Blessed Mother, the Christians won a great victory. In gratitude to Mary, St. Pius V established the feast of Our Lady of the Rosary. We celebrate it each year on October 7.

Pope Pius V died in Rome on May 1, 1572. His feast is celebrated today because May 1 is the feast of St. Joseph the Worker. Pius V was proclaimed a saint by Pope Clement XI in 1712.

Pope Pius V reminds us by his life that the Lord chooses us for reasons of his own. We are all so important to him because we are his creatures. All we have to do is keep the communication lines open between us and God. We do this by daily prayer, by receiving the sacraments of Eucharist and Reconciliation. We do this also by wise media viewing and listening. We do this by going places and choosing friends who are wholesome.

may

MAY 1

ST. JOSEPH THE WORKER

This is St. Joseph's second feast day on the Church calendar of celebrations. We honor him also on March 19. St. Joseph is a very important saint. He is the husband of Our Lady and the foster-father of Jesus.

Today we celebrate his witness of hard work. He was a carpenter who worked long hours in his little shop. St. Joseph teaches us that the work we do is important. Through it we give our contribution and our service to our family and society. But even more than that. As Christians we realize that our work is like a mirror of ourselves. That is why we want our work to be done with diligence.

Many countries set aside one day a year to honor workers. This encourages the dignity and appreciation of work. The Church has given us a wonderful model of work, St. Joseph. In 1955, Pope Pius XII proclaimed this feast of St. Joseph the Worker to be celebrated every year.

We can ask St. Joseph to help us become more diligent in our study and work.

MAY 2

ST. ATHANASIUS

Athanasius was born around 297 in Alexandria, Egypt. He devoted his life to proving that Jesus is truly God. This is important because some people called Arians denied it. Even before he became a priest, Athanasius had read many books on the faith. That is why he could so easily point out the false teachings of the Arians.

This saint became the archbishop of Alexandria when he was not yet thirty years old. For forty-six years, he was a brave shepherd of his flock. Four Roman emperors could not make him stop writing his clear and beautiful explanations of our holy faith. His enemies persecuted him in every way.

Five times he was sent out of his own diocese. His first exile lasted two years. He was sent to the city of Trier in 336. A kindly bishop, St. Maximinius, welcomed him warmly. The feast of St. Maximinius is celebrated on May 29. Other exiles lasted longer. Athanasius was hunted by people who wanted to kill him. During one tense exile, monks kept him safe in the desert for seven years. His enemies just could not find him.

Once the emperor's soldiers were chasing Athanasius down the Nile River. "They are catching up to us!" cried the saint's friends. Athanasius was not worried. "Turn the boat around," he said calmly, "and row toward them." The soldiers in the other boat shouted, "Have you seen Athanasius?" Back came the answer: "You are not far from him!" The enemy boat sped by them faster than ever, and the saint was safe!

The people of Alexandria loved their good archbishop. He was a real father to them. As the years passed, they appreciated more and more how much he had suffered for Jesus and the Church. It was the people who stepped in and saw to it that Athanasius had some well-deserved peace. He spent the last seven years of his life safe with them. His enemies hunted but could never find him. During that time, St. Athanasius wrote *The Life of St. Anthony the Hermit.* Anthony had been his personal friend when Athanasius was young. St. Anthony's feast is celebrated on January 17.

St. Athanasius died quietly on May 2, 373. He remains one of the greatest, bravest saints of all time.

This saint challenges us to be more energetic about studying our faith. We can ask St. Athanasius to give us some of his enthusiasm and love for Jesus.

ST. PHILIP AND ST. JAMES

Both of these saints were part of the original group of Jesus' twelve apostles. Philip was one of the first apostles chosen. He was born at Bethsaida, in Galilee. Our Lord found him and said, "Follow me." Philip was so happy to be with Jesus. He wanted to share his happiness with his friend, Nathaniel. "We have found the one Moses and the prophets wrote about," Philip explained. "He is Jesus of Nazareth."

Nathaniel was not at all excited. Nazareth was just a little village. It was not big and important like Jerusalem. So Nathaniel said, "Can any good come out of Nazareth?" But Philip did not become angry at his friend's answer. He just said, "Come and see." Nathaniel went to see Jesus. After he had spoken with him, he, too, became a zealous follower of the Lord.

St. James was also one of Jesus' twelve apostles. He was the son of Alpheus and a cousin of Our Lord. After Jesus ascended into heaven, James became the bishop of Jerusalem. People thought so much of him that they called him "James the Just," which means "James the Holy One." He is also called "James the Less," because he was younger than the other apostle named James. The other James was called "James the Greater" because he was older.

The saint of today's feast was very gentle and

forgiving. He prayed very much. He kept begging God to forgive the people who persecuted the followers of Jesus. Even when Our Lord's enemies were putting him to death, he asked God to pardon them. St. James died a martyr in the year 62.

We can all be apostles of Jesus in our own way. We can share the Good News of what faith in Jesus does for our lives. That is the way to imitate St. Philip and St. James.

MAY 4

BLESSED MARIE-LEONIE PARADIS

Elodie Paradis was born in the village of L'Acadie in Quebec, Canada. It was May 12, 1840. Her parents were poor but devout Catholics. They loved their little girl. When Elodie was nine, her parents decided to send her to a boarding school. They wanted her to have an excellent education. The Sisters of Notre Dame warmly received the new student. But Elodie and her family missed each other very much.

Mr. Paradis worked hard running a mill. But times were bad, and the mill did not produce enough to support his wife and children. He heard wonderful reports of the gold rush in California. He was so desperate that he decided to go. In California, Mr. Paradis did not find the wealth he hoped for. When he returned to L'Acadie, he was shocked to find that his Elodie had joined the convent. She had entered the Holy Cross congregation on February 21, 1854. Mr. Paradis went to the convent. He begged his daughter to return home, but she chose to remain. Finally, her father accepted it. She pronounced her vows in 1857. Blessed Marie-Leonie taught school in different cities. She prayed and lived her life joyfully.

As time went on, Sister Marie-Leonie was led by Jesus to begin a new religious order in the Church. The Little Sisters of the Holy Family were begun in 1880. These loving sisters are devoted to the priesthood. They serve priests in the household care so important to their ministry. The Little Sisters of the Holy Family now have sixty-seven convents in Canada, the United States, Rome and Honduras.

Mother Marie-Leonie worked for her sisters until the last few hours of her life. She was always frail and often ill. But she never stopped caring for God's people. She put the last corrections on the pages of the book of rules she had written. She had it sent to the print shop. That book would give her sisters the guidance they would need for their life. It was Friday, May 3, 1912. Mother Marie-Leonie said she felt very tired. She went to rest and died a few hours later. She was seventy-one years old.

Mother Marie-Leonie was declared "blessed" by Pope John Paul II. The joyful event took place at Jarry Park, Montreal, Canada, on September 11, 1984.

Sometimes we are afraid of failure or worried about our future. We can ask Blessed Marie-Leonie to help us be ready to listen to God's voice as she was.

ST. JUDITH OF PRUSSIA

St. Judith lived in the thirteenth century. She was born in Thuringia. This was in what is now central Germany. She wanted to model her life on the example of St. Elizabeth of Hungary. This saint's feast is celebrated on November 17. St. Elizabeth of Hungary had lived from 1207 until 1231. She had been proclaimed a saint in 1235. In St. Judith's time, many Christian women were influenced by her inspiring example.

Judith of Prussia was married at fifteen to a wealthy young nobleman. Judith tried to be a good Christian wife. She was especially generous with the poor. Her husband was a good man, but he was satisfied with his wealthy lifestyle. He expected his wife to dress and live like a rich woman. He felt that their well-dressed look would win them respect. But Judith gently persuaded him to live and dress more simply. By doing this, they would have more to give to people less fortunate than themselves.

Judith's husband died suddenly while on a pilgrimage to the Holy Land. The young widow raised her children alone. When the children grew up, Judith listened to a longing that had been in her heart during the busy, happy days of her life. She gave away everything and lived as a hermit. She moved to Prussia where people would not know that she was from a wealthy family. There she spent her time praying and taking care of weary travelers who passed by her little hut. She prayed especially for the conversion of nonbelievers. She prayed also for the newly baptized Christians to be true to their faith.

"Three things can lead us close to God," she once said. "They are painful physical suffering, being in exile in a foreign land, and being poor by choice because of love for God." St. Judith died of fever in 1260.

Whenever we start to worry about the impression we are making, we can pray to St. Judith. We can ask her to help us keep our sights on God. That is more important than worrying over what people say about us.

MAY 6

BLESSED FRANCOIS DE MONTMORENCY LAVAL

Blessed Francois was the first bishop of Quebec City, Canada. He was born in 1623 in a small town in France. Francois received a good, Catholic education. He studied with the Jesuits and then went to Paris to complete his preparation for the priesthood. Francois became a priest in May, 1647. He was consecrated a bishop on December 8, 1658, and arrived in New France in 1659.

Bishop Laval had a missionary spirit. He accepted the pioneer life of his people. Even more, Francois had the courage to take on a huge task. He was to organize the Church in Canada which was still mission territory. Bishop Laval asked the Jesuit missionaries to minister to the native people. He created new parishes for the French-speaking Catholics. He started the seminary of Quebec in 1663. This was of great importance because a good seminary would train future priests for God's people.

Bishop Laval loved the people of his vast territory. He was a caring bishop and a prayerful man. His particular cross was the constant interference by civil authorities. He was particularly outspoken about the harm of alcohol trafficking.

In 1688, he retired and was replaced by Bishop de Saint-Vallier. Bishop Laval devoted the last twenty years of his life to charitable and spiritual works. He died in 1708. Pilgrims prayed at his tomb and miracles were reported. Pope John Paul II declared Bishop Laval "blessed" on June 22, 1980.

Bishop Laval helps us become aware of what it means to be a missionary. He had the courage to leave his own country to go to Canada when it was still a mission land. We can ask Bishop Laval to make us aware of the Church all around the world. We can include people everywhere in our prayers.

MAY 7

BLESSED ROSE VENERINI

Blessed Rose was born in Viterbo, Italy, in 1656. Her father was a physician. Rose entered the convent but returned home after a few months. Her father had died and she felt the responsibility for taking care of her widowed mother.

Rose, who was to remain single, recognized her own leadership qualities. She gathered the young women in her neighborhood. They prayed the Rosary together in the evenings. As they all got to know each other, Rose became aware of how little the young people knew about their faith. Rose and two helpers opened a free school for girls in 1685. The parents who sent their daughters there were very pleased with the quality of education and the atmosphere.

Rose was a gifted educator. Above all, she was able to teach others to teach. In 1692, Cardinal Barbarigo invited Rose to his diocese. He wanted her to organize his schools and train his teachers. It was in his diocese that she became a friend and teacher of a future saint. That person was St. Lucy Filippini who started a religious order. Sister Lucy was proclaimed a saint in 1930.

Rose organized schools in various places. Some people resented her work and harassed her and her teachers. But the teachers held on to their belief in the value of education. Rose even opened a school in Rome in 1713. Pope Clement XI congratulated Rose for starting such a wonderful school.

This dedicated teacher died in Rome on May 7, 1728, at the age of seventy-two. After her death, Blessed Rose's lay teachers became religious sisters. The Venerini sisters continue to perform their teaching ministry the way Blessed Rose would. Rose Venerini was declared "blessed" by Pope Pius XII in 1952.

Blessed Rose realized the value of education. If we need to put more effort into our school work, we can ask Blessed Rose to help us.

MAY 8

BLESSED CATHERINE OF ST. AUGUSTINE

Catherine was born on May 3, 1632, in a little village in France. She was baptized the same day. Catherine's family were devout Catholics. Her grandparents set the example especially because of their genuine care for the poor. Catherine watched wide-eyed as her grandmother invited a handicapped beggar into her home. She offered him a bath, clean clothes and a delicious meal. As Catherine and her grandparents sat around the fire that night, they prayed the Our Father out loud. They thanked God for his blessings.

Because there was no hospital in their small French town, the sick were nursed back to health in the home of Catherine's grandparents. Catherine began to realize that sickness and suffering take patience. She was just a little girl but she prayed to ask Jesus to make people suffer less. When she was still quite young, she joined a new order of Sisters of St. Augustine. They took care of the sick in hospitals. She received the religious habit on October 24, 1646. That was the same day her older sister pronounced her vows. In 1648, Catherine listened to the missionary priests begging sisters to come to New France or Canada. It was missionary territory. Catherine's sister was chosen to be one of the first of their order to go as a missionary to Canada. Sister Catherine was just sixteen, but she begged to be chosen too. She pronounced her vows on May 4, 1648. Then she sailed for Canada the next day. It was the day before her sixteenth birthday.

Life was hard in Quebec, Canada. Sister Catherine loved the people. The Indians were so grateful for her cheerful ways. She cooked and cared for the sick in the order's poor hospital building. But Sister Catherine learned about fear, too. The Iroquois Indians were killing people and burning villages. She prayed to St. John Brebeuf, one of the Jesuit priests who had just been killed by the Iroquois in 1649. She asked him to help her be true to her calling. She heard him speaking in her heart, telling her to remain. Food became scarce and the winters were terribly cold. Some of the sisters could not take the harsh life and constant fear of death. Sadly they returned to France. Sister Catherine was afraid, too. Sometimes she could hardly pray. And while she smiled at all the dear people she cared for in the sick wards, she grew sad. It was then, when things were darkest for her, that she made a vow never to leave Canada. She promised to remain, performing her works of charity until death. When she made that vow she was just twenty-two years old.

Despite the hard pioneer life of the French colony, more people came. The Church grew. God blessed the new land with more missionaries. In 1665, Sister Catherine became the novice mistress of her community. She kept up her life of prayer and hospital ministry until her death. Sister Marie Catherine of St. Augustine died on May 8, 1668. She was thirty-six years old. She was declared "blessed" by Pope John Paul II in 1989.

Jesus never promised us that our lives would be easy and without pain or trouble. He did promise to be with us always. When we become afraid or downhearted, we can ask Blessed Catherine of St. Augustine to give us some of her courage.

MAY 9

BLESSED NICHOLAS ALBERGATI

Blessed Nicholas was born in Bologna, Italy. Nicholas' family could afford to send him to the university where he began to study law. But then after a few years, he decided not to become a lawyer. At the age of twenty, Nicholas joined the Carthusian order. In 1417, this Carthusian monk was chosen to be bishop of his native diocese. He had not counted on that at all. He could not even believe it could be God's will. But his superiors assured him it was.

People liked Bishop Nicholas. He lived in a small, plain house. He was like them. He began to visit the people of his diocese. He went to the poorest families first. He talked with them and helped them with their needs. He blessed their homes. The people were very grateful.

Bishop Nicholas became a cardinal in 1426. He was known to be wise and spiritual. Two popes, Martin V and Eugene IV, consulted him about important Church matters. Blessed Nicholas also encouraged learning. In fact, he wrote several books himself.

He died while on a visit to Siena, Italy. Pope Eugene IV had his body brought back to Bologna. The pope himself participated in the funeral Mass and burial.

Blessed Nicholas died in 1443.

Do you ever feel upset when you don't get attention? That is the time to pray to Blessed Nicholas. He kept receiving attention that he did not even want. Blessed Nicholas will show us how much better it is to spend our time praising God.

❧

MAY 10

ST. ANTONINUS

St. Antoninus lived in the fifteenth century. Even as a boy he showed that he had good sense and will power. The story is told that when he was fifteen, he asked to join the Dominican order. He looked young, and he was small. The prior studied him for a moment and then said, "I'll accept you when you know 'Gratian's Decree' by heart." "Gratian's Decree" was a book, several hundred pages long. So, in other words, the prior was telling Antoninus "no."

But Antoninus accepted the challenge. One year later he returned. It would be hard to describe the prior's amazement when he found that Antoninus had memorized the whole decree! Needless to say, he was accepted at once. (It was not his ability to memorize that changed the prior's mind, though. It was because he had proved he was serious about his vocation.)

Though just sixteen, Antoninus continued to surprise everyone by the way he lived the life of his order. As he grew older, he was given one important position after another. He was a good influence on his fellow Dominicans. They loved and respected him. This is proved powerfully in the life of Blessed Anthony Neyrot whose feast is April 10.

In March, 1446, Antoninus became the archbishop of Florence, Italy. "The father of the poor" was the name given this saint. He never refused to help anyone. When he had no more money, he would give his clothes, his shoes, his furniture or his one mule. Many times this mule was sold to help someone. Then it would be bought back for him by wealthy citizens. Of course, he would sell it again to help someone else!

Often St. Antoninus would say, "A successor of the apostles should not own anything except the wealth of virtue." St. Antoninus died in 1459. He was proclaimed a saint in 1523.

St. Antoninus will help us keep our priorities straight. He knew where he was going in life. He wanted to be true to his ideals until death. We can ask him to help us be as faithful to Jesus as he was.

MAY 11

ST. IGNATIUS OF LACONI

Ignatius was the son of a poor farmer in Laconi, Italy. He was born on December 17, 1701. When he was about seventeen, he became very ill. He promised to be a Franciscan if he would get better. But when the illness left him, his father convinced him to wait. A couple of years later, Ignatius was almost killed when he lost control of his horse. Suddenly, however, the horse stopped and trotted on quietly. Ignatius was convinced, then, that God had saved his life. He made up his mind to follow his religious vocation at once.

Brother Ignatius never had any important position in the Franciscan order. For fifteen years he worked in the weaving shed. Then, for forty years, he was part of the team who went out from house to house. They requested food and donations to support the friars. Ignatius visited families and received their gift. But the people soon realized that they received a gift in return. Brother Ignatius consoled the sick and cheered up the lonely. He made peace between enemies, converted people hardened by sin and advised those in trouble. They began to wait for his visits.

There were some difficult days, too. Once in a while, a door was slammed in his face, and often the weather was bad. Always, there were miles and miles to walk. But Ignatius was dedicated. Yet people noticed he used to skip one house. The owner was a rich moneylender. He made the poor pay back much more than they could afford. This man felt humiliated because Ignatius never visited his home to ask for donations. He complained to Brother Ignatius' superior. The superior knew nothing about the moneylender so he sent Ignatius to his home. Brother Ignatius never said a word, but did as he was told. He returned with a large sack of food. It was then that God worked a miracle. When the sack was emptied, blood dripped out. "This is the blood of the poor," Ignatius explained softly. "That is why I never ask for anything at that house." The friars began to pray that the moneylender would repent.

Brother Ignatius died at the age of eighty, on May 11, 1781. He was proclaimed a saint by Pope Pius XII in 1951.

Brother Ignatius was a happy, dedicated Franciscan. He makes us realize that the best gift we can give anyone is a good example.

ST. NEREUS, ST. ACHILLEUS AND ST. PANCRAS

Nereus and Achilleus were Roman soldiers who died around 304. They were probably Praetorian guards under Emperor Trajan. We know little else about them. But what we do know comes from two popes who lived in the fourth century, Pope Siricius and Pope Damasus. In 398, Pope Siricius built a church in their honor in Rome. Pope Damasus wrote a brief tribute to the martyrs. He explained that Nereus and Achilleus were converted to the Christian faith. They left behind their weapons forever. They were true followers of Jesus even at the cost of their own lives. Nereus and Achilleus were sent into exile to the island of Terracina. There they were beheaded. In the sixth century, a second church was built in another part of Rome to honor these two martyrs.

St. Pancras, a fourteen-year-old orphan, lived at the same time. He could possibly have been killed on the same day. Pancras was not a native of Rome. He was brought there by his uncle who looked after him. He became a follower of Jesus and was baptized. Although just a boy, he was arrested for being a Christian. Pancras refused to give up his faith. For that, he was sentenced to death. Pancras was beheaded. He became a very popular martyr in the early Church. People admired him for being so young and so brave. In 514, a large church was built in Rome to honor him. In 596, the famous missionary, St. Augustine of Canterbury, went to bring the Christian faith to England. He named his first church there after St. Pancras.

The martyrs of Rome remind us of the importance of our Catholic faith. It should mean as much to us as it did to each of them. If we need our faith strengthened, we can ask Nereus, Achilleus and Pancras to help us.

MAY 13

ST. ANDREW FOURNET

St. Andrew Fournet was born on December 6, 1752. He was from Maille, a little town near Poitiers, in France. Andrew's parents were religious people. Mrs. Fournet had her heart set on Andrew becoming a priest. The little boy heard this more often than he cared to. Once he declared, "I'm a good boy, but I'm still not going to be a priest or monk."

When he grew up, he went to Poitiers to study college subjects. But that did not last long. He was having too good of a time. His mother followed him and steered him to good occupations. But they fell through, one after another. His mother was frantic. There was only one more possibility. She talked Andrew into going to stay for a while with his uncle, a priest. His uncle's parish was poor and his uncle was a holy man. For some unpredictable reason, Andrew agreed. This was God's "teachable moment."

Andrew's uncle recognized his nephew's good qualities. His own example sparked something in Andrew and he settled down. He began to study seriously and to make up for lost time. He was ordained a priest and was assigned to his uncle's parish. In 1781, he was transferred to his home parish in Maille. His mother was jubilant. He had become a caring, prayerful priest.

When the French Revolution began, St. Andrew refused to take an oath that was against the Church. He became a hunted man. In 1792, he was forced to flee to Spain. There he remained for five years. But he worried about his people and went back to France. The danger was as great as before. Father Fournet was protected by his flock. He nearly escaped death several times. Meanwhile, he heard confessions, celebrated the Eucharist, gave the Last Rites.

When the Church was free again, St. Andrew came out of hiding. He was always inviting his people to love and serve God. One of the good ladies from the area, St. Elizabeth Bichier des Ages, helped St. Andrew very much. Together they started an order of sisters called the Daughters of the Cross. St. Elizabeth's feast day is August 26.

St. Andrew died on May 13, 1834, at the age of eighty-two. He was proclaimed a saint by Pope Pius XI on June 4, 1933.

When we need more courage or more energy, we can ask St. Andrew Fournet to help us.

ST. MATTHIAS

St. Matthias was one of Our Lord's seventy-two disciples. He had been a follower of Jesus during his public life. St. Peter asked the 120 people gathered in prayer to choose an apostle to replace Judas. This was very important because that man would be a bishop, as the other apostles were. He said it should be someone who had been with Jesus from his baptism in the Jordan until the resurrection.

The first chapter of the Acts of the Apostles explains that the group proposed two names. One was Matthias, the other, Joseph, called Barsabbas. Joseph was also called Justus. Both men—Matthias and Joseph—were very well thought of by Jesus' followers. So now they had two replacements for Judas. But they only needed one. So what could they do? It was very simple. They cast lots. Matthias' name was chosen.

St. Matthias was a very good apostle. He preached the Good News in Judea. Then he continued to Cappadocia (modern-day Turkey). Many people listened to Matthias. They believed his wonderful message. The enemies of Jesus grew furious to see how people listened to Matthias. They decided to stop him. Matthias died a martyr.

St. Matthias reminds us that we are fortunate to be

followers of Jesus and members of his Church. Let us ask St. Matthias to show us how to be more grateful for what we have received.

MAY 15

ST. ISIDORE THE FARMER

This saint was born in 1070, in Madrid, Spain. His parents were deeply religious. They named their son after the great St. Isidore, archbishop of Seville, Spain. We celebrate his feast on April 4. Isidore's parents wanted to offer their son a first-rate education, but they could not afford it. They were tenant farmers. Their son would spend his life in the same occupation.

Isidore went to work for a rich land owner in Madrid. The man's name was John de Vargas. Isidore worked all his life for Mr. de Vargas. He married a good girl from a family as poor as his own. The couple loved each other very much. They had one child, a boy, who died as a baby. Isidore and his wife offered to Jesus their sadness over the child's death. They trusted their son was happy with God forever.

St. Isidore began each day at Mass. Then he would go to his job. He tried to work hard even if he didn't feel like it. He plowed and planted and prayed. He called on Mary, the saints and his guardian angel. They helped him turn ordinary days into special, joyful times. The world of faith became very real to St. Isidore, as real as Mr. de Vargas' fields. When he had a day off, Isidore made it a point to spend extra time adoring Jesus in church. Sometimes, on holidays, Isidore and his wife would visit a few neighboring parishes on a one-day pilgrimage of prayer.

Once the parish had a dinner. Isidore arrived early and went into the church to pray. He arrived in the parish hall late. He didn't come in alone. He brought a group of beggars, too. The parishioners were upset. What if there wasn't enough food for all those beggars? But the more they filled up their plates, the more there was for everybody else. St. Isidore said kindly, "There is always enough for the poor of Jesus."

Stories of miracles began to circulate about this farm-worker saint. Isidore was totally unselfish. He was a loving and compassionate human being. He is one of Spain's most popular saints. Isidore died on May 15, 1130. In March, 1622, Pope Gregory XV proclaimed five great saints together. They were St. Ignatius Loyola, St. Francis Xavier, St. Teresa of Avila, St. Philip Neri and St. Isidore the Farmer.

St. Isidore let his faith in Jesus and the Church light up his whole life. We can ask him to help us love the Lord as he did.

ST. UBALD

This saint lived in twelfth-century Italy. He was an orphan raised by his uncle, a bishop. Ubald was given a good education. When he finished his schooling, he had the chance to marry. But he became a priest instead. Eventually, the pope made him bishop of Gubbio, the city of his birth.

St. Ubald became well-known for his mild and patient disposition. One time, for example, a worker was repairing the city wall. He badly damaged the bishop's vineyard. The saint gently pointed it out to him. The workman must have been very tired. He probably did not even recognize the bishop. He shoved Bishop Ubald so hard that he fell into a pile of wet cement. He was covered with it. He got up, cleaned himself off and went into the house. Some people saw the whole thing and demanded that the worker be brought to court. Bishop Ubald appeared in the courtroom and obtained the man's freedom.

The holy bishop loved peace and he had the courage it takes to keep it. Once, when the people of Gubbio were fighting in the streets, he threw himself between the two angry crowds. He seemed unafraid of the swords clashing and the rocks flying. Suddenly he fell to the ground. The people stopped fighting at once. They thought the bishop had been killed. But he got up. He showed them he was not even hurt. The people thanked God. They stopped fighting and went home.

Another time, Emperor Frederick Barbarossa was on his way to attack Gubbio. St. Ubald did not wait for him and his army to come to the city. He went out on the road to talk to him. No one knows what he said. All they know is that he convinced the emperor to leave Gubbio alone.

The saint had a great amount of physical pain. Yet he never talked about it. On Easter Sunday, 1160, he rose for Mass. He gave a beautiful sermon and blessed the people. Then he had to go back to bed. He was not able to get up again. He died on May 16, 1160. All the people came to pay their respects. They cried and prayed to St. Ubald to take care of them from heaven.

It is easy to become angry at times. And it is hard to forgive others when they hurt us. We can pray to St. Ubald. We can ask to be meek and forgiving as he was.

❦

MAY 17

ST. PASCHAL BAYLON

Paschal, a Spanish saint, was born in 1540. From the time he was seven, he worked as a shepherd. He never had the opportunity to go to school. Yet he taught himself to read and write. He did this mainly by asking everyone he met to help him. This he did so that he could read from religious books. He used to whisper prayers often during the day as he took care of the sheep.

When he was twenty-four, the shepherd became a Franciscan brother. His companions liked him. Paschal was easy to get along with and kind. The community noticed that he often did the most unpleasant and hardest chores. He practiced penances that were even more strict than the rule required. Yet he was a happy person. When he had been a shepherd, he had wished he could be in church praying to Jesus. But he couldn't. Now he could. He loved to keep the Lord company in the Blessed Sacrament. He was also honored to be a server at Mass.

St. Paschal's two great loves were the Holy Eucharist and the Blessed Mother. Every day Paschal prayed the Rosary with great love. He also wrote beautiful prayers to our Heavenly Mother.

Out of some scraps of paper, St. Paschal made himself a little notebook. In it, he wrote down some beautiful thoughts and prayers. After he died, his superior showed the little book to the local archbishop. He read the book and said, "These simple souls are stealing heaven from us!"

Paschal died in 1592 at the age of fifty-two. He was proclaimed a saint by Pope Alexander VIII in 1690.

What does it take to be a saint? Pascal Baylon lived his religious vocation as best he could. He had the strength to do that, though, because of his devotion to Jesus in the Holy Eucharist and to the Blessed Mother. We can ask St. Pascal to help us grow closer to Jesus in the Eucharist and to Mary.

ST. JOHN I

John I was a priest of Rome. He became pope after the death of Pope St. Hormisdas in 523. At that time, Italy's ruler, Theodoric the Goth, was an Arian. (The Arians did not believe that Jesus is God.) Theodoric let Catholics alone at the beginning of his reign. Later, however, he changed and became arrogant and suspicious of everyone. He imagined there was a conspiracy against him. After a while, he believed the whole world was out to get his throne and his power. The one person who most certainly did not want either was the pope.

Theodoric was trying to get Pope John involved in his political problems. The emperor was having trouble with Emperor Justin I of Constantinople. It had been reported that Justin was being too hard on the Arians in the east. Theodoric sent a delegation to negotiate with Justin. The delegation was headed by Pope John I. Emperor Justin received the pope and his companions with rejoicing. Justin was very willing to change his harsh policy. Pope John's mission went very well. But Emperor Theodoric was not pleased. He imagined that Pope John and Justin I were against him. The pope was returning to Rome and got as far as Ravenna, Theodoric's capital. Pope John was kidnapped and thrown into prison by Theodoric's soldiers. There the pope died of thirst and starvation in 526.

Do you ever find yourself thinking mean thoughts about people? That is when we can pray to Pope St. John I. He will help us avoid Theodoric's terrible mistake of letting our actions follow from jealous, untrue thoughts. Pope St. John I will lead us to be heroic Christians as he was.

❦

MAY 19

ST. CELESTINE V

Peter di Morone was the eleventh of twelve children. He was born around 1210 in Isernia, Italy. His father died when he was small. The family was poor, but Peter's mother raised her children with great love. She sent Peter to school because he showed such promise and an eagerness to learn. Once she asked as usual, "Which one of you is going to become a saint?" Little Peter who was to become Pope Celestine answered with all his heart, "Me, Mama! I'll become a saint!" And he did. But it wasn't easy.

When he was twenty, Peter became a hermit. He spent his days praying, reading the Bible and doing his work. Other hermits kept coming to him and asking him to guide them. Eventually, he started a new order of monks.

When Peter was eighty-four years of age, he was made pope. It came about in a very unusual way. For two years there had been no pope. This was because the cardinals could not agree on whom to choose. Peter sent them a message. He warned them to decide quickly, because God was not pleased with the long delay. The cardinals did as the monk said. Then and there, they chose Peter the hermit to be pope! The poor man wept when he heard the news. He accepted sadly and took the name Celestine V.

He was pope only about five months. Because he was so humble and simple, people took advantage of him. He could not say "no" to anyone. Soon there was great confusion. Pope Celestine felt very responsible for all the trouble. He decided that the best thing he could do for the Church was give up his position. He did so. He asked forgiveness for not having governed the Church well.

All St. Celestine wanted was to live in one of his monasteries in peace. But the new pope, Boniface VIII, thought it would be safer to keep him hidden in a small room in one of the Roman palaces. St. Celestine spent the last ten months of his life in a plain cell-like room. But he became his cheerful self again. "All you wanted was a cell, Peter," he would repeat to himself. "Well, you've got it." He died on May 19, 1296. He was proclaimed a saint by Pope Clement VI in 1313.

St. Celestine was a great monk. The way he handled his painful time as pope proved that he really was holy. He shows us that when we do our best at something, we can leave the results up to God and be in peace.

MAY 20

ST. BERNARDINE OF SIENA

St. Bernardine of Siena was born in 1380 in a town near Siena, Italy. He was the son of an Italian governor. His parents died when he was seven. His relatives loved him as if he were their own. They also gave him a good education. He grew up to be a tall, handsome boy. He was so much fun that his friends loved to be with him. Yet they knew better than to use any dirty words when he was around. He would not put up with it. Twice when a man tried to lead him into sin, Bernardine punched him and sent him on his way.

The saint had a special love for the Blessed Mother. She was the one who kept him pure. Even when he was a teenager, Bernardine would pray to her as a child talks with his mother.

Bernardine was tender-hearted. He felt great pity for the poor. Once, his aunt had no extra food to give a beggar. The boy cried, "I'd rather go without food myself than leave that poor man with none." When a plague struck the area in 1400, Bernardine and his friends volunteered their services at the hospital. They helped the sick and dying day and night for six weeks until the plague had ended.

Bernardine joined the Franciscan order when he was twenty-two. He became a priest. After several years, he was assigned to go to towns and cities to preach. The people needed to be reminded about the love of Jesus. In those days, bad habits were ruining both young and old people. "How can I save these people by myself?" Bernardine asked the Lord in prayer. "With what weapons can I fight the devil?" And God answered, "My Holy Name will be enough for you." So Bernardine spread devotion to the Holy Name of Jesus. He used this Name a great many times in every sermon. He asked people to print Jesus' Name over the gates of their cities, over their doorways—everywhere. Through devotion to the Holy Name of Jesus and devotion to the Blessed Mother, Bernardine brought thousands of people from all over Italy back to the Church.

St. Bernardine spent forty-two years of his life as a Franciscan. He died at the age of sixty-four in Aquila, Italy. It was May 20, 1444. He was declared a saint just six years later, in 1450, by Pope Nicholas V.

Bernardine really cared about people. He turned all his joy and energy into serving Jesus and making everyone love his Holy Name. We can pray often, "Blessed be the Name of Jesus."

MAY 21

BLESSED EUGENE DE MAZENOD

Eugene was born in France in 1782. He became a priest in 1811. Father Eugene was sensitive to the needs of the poor and he ministered to them. He was always eager to find new ways to reach out to the young. He wanted to bring them to the love and practice of their faith. He believed in the value of parish missions. He realized that missionary priests in a parish could do so much good to reawaken in people dedication to their faith.

Father de Mazenod began a new religious order of priests and lay brothers in 1826. They were missionaries called the Oblates of Mary Immaculate. Their particular ministry was to go to people who had never heard of Jesus and his Church. Father de Mazenod and his order were courageous in answering the requests of bishops who needed their help. Bishops of North America eagerly awaited the Oblates. Bishop Ignace Bourget of Montreal was especially eager. He must have been very convincing because the founder sent several of his members. Within ten years, the Oblates had grown rapidly. They reached all of Canada and had begun to minister in the United States, too.

In 1837, Father de Mazenod was consecrated bishop of Marseilles, France. He became known for his loyalty and love for the pope. He was also a gifted organizer and educator. Bishop de Mazenod remained superior of his order until he died in 1861.

The great work Bishop de Mazenod started continues today through the Oblate missionaries around the world. They staff mission posts, parishes and universities.

Bishop de Mazenod had the courage to respond to the needs of God's people as he saw them. We can ask Bishop de Mazenod to give us an awareness of how we, too, can help the people around us.

ST. RITA OF CASCIA

Rita was born in 1381 in a little Italian village. Her parents were older. They had begged God to send them a child. They brought Rita up well. Rita wanted to enter the convent when she was fifteen, but her parents decided that she should marry instead. The man they chose for Rita turned out to be a mean and unfaithful husband. He had such a violent temper that everyone in the neighborhood was afraid of him. Yet, for eighteen years, his wife patiently took all his insults. Her prayers, gentleness and goodness finally won his heart. He apologized to Rita for the way he had treated her and he returned to God.

Rita's happiness over her husband's conversion did not last long. One day, shortly after, he was murdered. Rita was shocked and heart-broken. But she forgave the murderers, and tried to make her two sons forgive them, too. She saw that the boys, instead, were determined to avenge their father's death. Rita prayed that they would die rather than commit murder. Within several months, both boys became seriously ill. Rita nursed them lovingly. During their illness, she pursuaded them to forgive, and to ask God's forgiveness for themselves. They did and both died peacefully.

Now her husband and her children were dead. Left alone in the world, Rita tried three times to enter the convent in Cascia. The rules of the convent did not permit a woman who had been married to join even if her husband had died. Rita did not give up, however. At last, the nuns made an exception for her. In the convent, Rita was outstanding for her obedience and charity. She had great devotion to the crucified Jesus. Once, while praying, she asked him to let her share some of his pain. One thorn from his crown of thorns pierced her forehead and made a sore that never healed. In fact, it grew so bad and gave off such an odor that St. Rita had to stay away from the others. She was happy to suffer to show her love for Jesus.

St. Rita died on May 22, 1457, when she was seventy-six. Like St. Jude, St. Rita is often called "Saint of the Impossible."

Maybe someone we know and love is not living close to God. We can ask St. Rita to help that person. We can ask her also to help us know how to pray for that person.

ST. JOHN BAPTIST ROSSI

John Baptist Rossi was born in 1698 in a village near Genoa, Italy. His family loved him. They were proud when a wealthy couple visiting their town offered to educate him. His parents knew the couple and trusted them. John was happy to be able to go to their house in Genoa because then he could attend school. Everything was going well for John. He became a student for the priesthood at the Roman College. He realized that studies were easy for him and took on more and more of a load.

John became very sick and had to stop his studies for a while. After he recovered enough, he completed his preparation and became a priest. Even though his health was always poor, Father John did so much good for the people of Rome. He knew what it was like not to feel well, so Father Rossi took a special interest in sick people. He was a frequent visitor in Rome's hospitals. He especially loved to spend time with the poor people at the Hospice of St. Galla. This was a shelter for the poor and homeless. But Father Rossi became aware of poor people who had no one to look after their spiritual needs. He noticed those who brought cattle and sheep to sell in the Roman forum. What hard lives they had. They came in the morning with their herds. Father Rossi would walk among them and stop and talk with them.

When possible, he would teach them about the faith and offer them the sacrament of Reconciliation. Father Rossi's priestly ministry made a big difference in their lives.

The priest also felt deep compassion for the homeless women and girls. They wandered through the streets day and night begging. This was dangerous and very sad. The pope gave Father Rossi money to open a shelter for homeless women. It was right near the Hospice of St. Galla. Father Rossi placed the house under the protection of one of his favorite saints, Aloysius Gonzaga. The feast of St. Aloysius is June 21. Father Rossi became best known for his kindness and gentleness in confession. People formed lines near his confessional and waited patiently for their turn. He once said to a friend that the best way for a priest to reach heaven was to help people through the sacrament of Reconciliation. Another favorite assignment given him by Pope Benedict XIV was to teach courses of spiritual instruction to prison officials and state employees.

Father Rossi suffered a stroke in 1763. He never regained his health. He was able to celebrate Mass but he suffered greatly. This wonderful priest died at the age of sixty-six. It was May 23, 1764. He was proclaimed a saint by Pope Leo XIII in 1881.

We can learn from the life of St. John Baptist Rossi to be grateful for priests. We can also pray to this saint and ask him to console priests for all the good they do.

ST. DAVID I OF SCOTLAND

David was born in 1080. He was the youngest son of St. Margaret, queen of Scotland, and her good husband, King Malcom. David himself became king when he was about forty. Those who knew him well saw how little he wanted to accept the royal crown. But once he was king, he was a very good one.

St. David ruled his kingdom with great justice. He was very charitable to the poor. All of his subjects were free to visit him whenever they desired. He gave everyone a good example with his own love of prayer. Under this holy king, the people of Scotland united more closely into one nation. They became better Christians.

King David established new dioceses. He built many new monasteries. He gave much money to the Church during his rule of about twenty years.

Two days before he died, he received the last sacraments. He spent his time praying with those attending him. The next day, they urged him to rest. King David answered, "Let me think about the things of God, instead, so that my soul may be strengthened on its trip from exile to home." By home, the saint meant our heavenly home. "When I stand before God's judgment seat, you will not be able to answer for me or defend me," he said. "No one will be able to deliver me from his hand." So he kept on praying right up until he died. St. David died on May 24, 1153.

We can be tempted to excuse our faults by saying "Everyone else does it." But we know that this excuse will not count when we stand before God to be judged. We can ask St. David to help us be as honest as he was in our relationship with God.

MAY 25

The current Roman calendar lists three saints on May 25. Their stories are briefly presented here, one after another.

❧

VENERABLE BEDE

This English priest is famous as a saint, a priest, a monk, a teacher and a writer of history. He was born in England in 673. His parents sent Bede to the local Benedictine monastery to receive an education. He loved the life of the monks so much that when he grew up he became a monk. He remained in that same monastery for the rest of his life.

St. Bede loved the Holy Bible very much. He tells us that it was a joy for him to study the Bible. He loved to teach it and write about it. When he grew older, sickness at last forced him to stay in bed. His pupils came to study by his bedside. He kept on teaching them and working on his translation of St. John's Gospel into English. Many people could not read Latin. He wanted them to be able to read the words of Jesus in their own language.

As he grew sicker, St. Bede realized that he was about to go back to God. The monks would miss him very much. He kept on working even when he was seriously ill. At last, the boy who was doing the writing for him said, "There is still one sentence, dear Father, which is not written down." "Write it quickly," answered the saint. When the boy said, "It is finished," the saint said, "Good! You are right—it is finished. Now please hold my head up. I want to sit facing the place where I used to pray. I want to call on my Heavenly Father."

St. Bede died shortly after, on May 25, 735. His most famous book, *Church History of the English People*, is the only source for much of early English history. People call Bede by the respectful title of "venerable." He is also a Doctor of the Church.

If Venerable Bede were alive now, how much time do you think he would spend every day watching TV? How much time do you spend daily watching TV? What adjustments might you make to allow time for important things like study, enrichment reading, household responsibilities, and so on?

ST. GREGORY VII

This pope's name was Hildebrand. He was born in Italy around 1023. His uncle was a monk in Rome so Hildebrand went to the monastery to be educated. Later, Hildebrand became a Benedictine monk in France. Soon, however, he was called back to Rome. There he held very important positions under several popes until he himself was made pope.

For twenty-five years, he had refused to let himself be elected. But when Pope Alexander II died, the cardinals made up their minds to elect Hildebrand pope. With one voice they cried out: "Hildebrand is the elect of St. Peter!" "They carried me to the throne," the saint wrote afterward. "My protests did no good. Fear filled my heart and darkness was all around me." Hildebrand chose the name Gregory VII.

These were truly dark times for the Catholic Church. Kings and emperors were interfering in Church matters. They named the men they wanted to be bishops, cardinals and even popes. Many of those appointed were not very good men. They were bad examples to the people.

The first thing Pope St. Gregory did was to spend several days in prayer. He also asked others to pray for him. He realized that without prayer nothing can be done well for God. Afterward, he began to act to make the clergy better. He also took steps to keep civil rulers out of the affairs of the Church. This was very difficult because the rulers were all against the change. However, some gave in.

One ruler, Emperor Henry IV of Germany, caused Pope Gregory great sufferings. This young man was sinful and greedy for gold. He would not stop trying to run the affairs of the Church. He even sent his men to capture the pope. But the people of Rome rescued the saint from prison. Pope Gregory excommunicated the emperor. That did nothing to stop Henry IV. He chose his own pope. Of course, the man he chose was not the real pope. But Henry tried to make people think he was. Then, once again, the emperor sent his armies to capture the saint. Pope Gregory was forced to leave Rome. He was taken safely to Salerno where he died in 1085. His last words were, "I have loved justice and hated evil. That is why I am dying in exile." He was proclaimed a saint by Pope Paul V in 1606.

Pope Gregory VII (Hildebrand) is known for his tremendous personal courage. He stood up for the cause of Jesus and his Church. If we want to be serious Christians today, we too will have to be courageous. This saint got his courage by praying. We can do the same.

ST. MARY MAGDALEN DE PAZZI

Catherine de Pazzi was born in Florence, Italy, in 1566. She was the only daughter of very rich parents. When she was fourteen, Catherine became a boarder at a convent school. There she grew to love life in a religious house. But about a year later, her father took her home. He began to think of choosing a rich husband for her. However, Catherine's heart was set on becoming a nun. She shocked her parents by telling them she had already made a vow of chastity. They could not believe it. Finally, they let her enter the Carmelite convent. Only fifteen days later, however, they came and took her home. They hoped to make her change her mind. After three months of trying, they gave up. They let her go back for good, with their blessing. It was 1582, the year St. Teresa of Avila died in Spain.

As a novice, St. Mary Magdalen became very sick. The nuns feared she might die. She was permitted to pronounce her religious vows. Since she was suffering greatly, one of the sisters asked her how she could stand that pain without a word. The saint pointed to the crucifix. She said: "See what the great love of God has suffered for my salvation. This same love sees my weakness and gives me strength."

St. Mary Magdalen had great sufferings her whole life. She also had very strong temptations to impurity and to greed for food. She overcame everything by her great love for Jesus in the Holy Eucharist and for Mary. Often she ate only bread and water. She practiced other acts of self-denial, too. Moreover, her love for Jesus became so great that she would say, "Love is not loved, not known by his own creatures." With tears, she would pray and offer her pains for sinners and unbelievers, right up until she died. She once said: "O my Jesus, if I had a voice loud and strong enough to be heard in every part of the world, I would cry out to make you known and loved by everyone!"

St. Mary Magdalen de Pazzi died on May 25, 1607, at the age of forty-one. She was proclaimed a saint by Pope Clement IX in 1669.

We can find it helpful to look at a crucifix from time to time. This makes us grow convinced of Jesus' love for us. We can pray, "My Jesus, I love you. Thank you for dying for me."

MAY 26

ST. PHILIP NERI

St. Philip Neri was born in Florence, Italy, in 1515. As a child, his nickname was "Good little Phil." He was always so jolly and friendly that everyone he met loved him. Philip went to Rome as a teenager. He studied theology and philosophy for three years and was a good student. Above all,

Philip was a very active Christian. He lived simply and worked hard. But he also did much good for the people around him. He helped poor children. He donated his time to the sick. He was a friend to people who were troubled and lonely. In fact, he reached out to everybody he could for the love of Jesus.

Philip helped start an organization of lay people to take care of needy pilgrims. That ministry gradually continued as a famous Roman hospital. The priest who guided him realized that Philip was doing so much to help the Christians of Rome become fervent again. But it became obvious when Philip was thirty-six that he had the call to be a priest. It was then that he began his most wonderful ministry for others. He started to hear confessions. He was available for the sacrament of Reconciliation for several hours every day. The lines of people who came to him grew longer. But Father Philip was never in a hurry. He never ran out of patience and gentleness.

People began to notice that he could read their minds at times. He could, in some circumstances, foretell the future. The Lord even worked miracles through him. But all Philip wanted to do was bring Jesus to the people. To avoid their admiration, he acted silly once in a while. He wanted people to laugh and forget that they thought he was holy.

St. Philip was making a difference, though. Because of him, the whole city of Rome was becoming better. Once he started to think about being a missionary to far-off lands. He was very impressed by the life of St. Francis Xavier, who had died in 1552 at the gate of China. Philip had just been one year a priest at the time of St. Xavier's death. Should he leave Rome and volunteer for the missions? A holy Cistercian monk told him "Rome is to be your mission land." After that, Father Philip was at peace.

St. Philip spent the last five years of his life offering the sacrament of Reconciliation to the people. He died at the age of eighty in 1595. He was proclaimed a saint by Pope Gregory XV in 1622.

How can we become more cheerful and generous? Isn't that what we all really want to be? We can say a little prayer to St. Philip Neri. He will share with us his secret of how to be happy.

MAY 27

ST. AUGUSTINE OF CANTERBURY

St. Augustine was the abbot of St. Andrew's monastery in Rome. Pope St. Gregory the Great chose him and forty other monks for a mission dear to his heart. They were to preach the Gospel to the people of England. Abbot Augustine and the monks started on their journey. When they reached southern France, people warned them that the English were fierce. The monks felt discouraged. They asked Augustine to go back to obtain the pope's permission to give up the whole idea. They did, but the pope asked them to go to England just the same. He said that the people wanted to accept the Christian faith. The monks went to England. They arrived in 596.

The missionaries were well received by King Ethelbert, whose wife was a Christian princess from France. The monks formed a procession when they landed. They walked along singing psalms. They carried a cross and a picture of Our Lord. Many people received the monks' message. King Ethelbert himself was baptized on Pentecost, 597. Abbot Augustine became a bishop that same year.

St. Augustine often wrote to ask the pope advice. And Pope St. Gregory gave him much holy advice, too. Speaking about the many miracles St. Augustine worked, the pope said: "You must rejoice with fear and fear with joy for that gift." He meant that Augustine should be happy that through the miracles the English were being converted. But he should be careful not to become proud.

At Canterbury, St. Augustine built a church and a monastery, which became the most important in England. It was there that he was buried. St. Augustine died seven years after his arrival in England, on May 26, 605.

When we are told to do something by our parents or those in authority, we should do it. If the task seems hard or we don't like it, we can ask St. Augustine of Canterbury to help us.

BLESSED MARGARET POLE

Blessed Margaret was born in 1471. She was the niece of two English kings, Edward IV and Richard III. Henry VII arranged her marriage to Sir Reginald Pole. He was a brave soldier and a friend of the royal family. By the time King Henry VIII came into power, Margaret was a widow with five children. The young Henry VIII was new to the throne and new to power. He called Margaret the holiest woman in England. He was so impressed with her that he returned some property her family had lost in the past. He also made her a countess.

Henry trusted her so much that Countess Margaret was appointed the governess of Princess Mary, his and Queen Catherine's daughter. But then Henry tried to marry Anne Boleyn although he already had a wife. Margaret did not approve of the king's behavior. The king made her leave the court. He let her know he was very displeased with her. The king was even more upset when one of Margaret's sons, a priest, wrote a long article against Henry's claim to be head of the Church in England. (Her son was to become the famous Cardinal Reginald Pole.) Henry was out of control. He had become cruel and hateful. He threatened to get rid of Margaret's whole family.

Henry sent people to question Countess Margaret. They were supposed to prove that she was a traitor. They questioned her from noon until evening. She never made any mistakes. She had nothing to hide. Margaret was kept under house arrest at the castle of a nobleman. Then she was moved to the huge tower of London. She never even had a trial. During the long winter months, she suffered very much from the cold and dampness. She had no fire and not enough warm clothing.

Finally, on May 28, 1541, Blessed Margaret was led out of the tower to the place of execution. She was tired and sick, but she stood tall and proud to die for her faith. "I am no traitor," she said courageously. Margaret was beheaded. She was seventy years old.

When we feel cowardly about a decision we have made for God, that's the time to call on Blessed Margaret Pole. We can ask her to make us courageous as she was.

MAY 29

ST. MAXIMINIUS

Maximinius was a bishop who lived in the fourth century. It is believed that he was born in Poitiers, France. As a young man, he heard of a saintly bishop of Trier, in Gaul. He traveled to that city and became a disciple of St. Agritius. This holy bishop saw to it that Maximinius received a thorough education. After several years of study and preparation, Maximinius became a priest and then bishop. He took over the diocese of Trier. Bishop Agritius could not have been more pleased. He knew that his people would have a wonderful bishop.

Maximinius lived in exciting times. All you have to do is read the May 2 saint's life to understand. When St. Athanasius of Alexandria, Egypt, was sent into exile to Trier, it was St. Maximinius who welcomed him. He did everything to help Athanasius and to make his time away from his people less painful. Another brave bishop of those times, St. Paul, bishop of Constantinople, was also protected by Maximinius from the wrath of Emperor Constantius.

St. Athanasius wrote that Maximinius was courageous and holy. He said that Maximinius was even well known as a miracle worker. Although it is believed that this bishop wrote much, his works have been lost. But what remains is the memory of his dedication to Jesus and to the Church. Because he was a great man, he was willing to stand up against those who persecuted the Church. He was willing also to protect those brave bishops who fell out of favor with the political powers. Maximinius put his own life on the line even if it meant loss of position or even his life, if necessary. He died around the year 347.

Did you ever see someone at school being picked on or left out? If you want to imitate St. Maximinius, be a friend to that person. You will find that God will treat you the same way.

ST. JOAN OF ARC

Joan was born in 1412. Her hometown was Domremy, a little village in France. Jacques d'Arc, her father, was a hard working farmer. Her mother was gentle and loving. She taught Joan many practical things. "I can sew and spin as well as any woman," she once said. Joan loved to pray, especially at the shrines of Our Blessed Mother. This honest little peasant girl was to become a heroine. One day while she was watching her sheep, St. Michael the Archangel, the patron of her country, told her, "Daughter of God, go save France!" For three years she heard the voices of saints calling her to action. When she was sixteen, she began her mission.

At that time, there was a war going on between France and England. It was called the Hundred Years' War. England had won so much French land that the king of England called himself the king of France, too. The real French king was weak and fun-loving. He thought the French armies would never be able to save the country.

With his permission, St. Joan led an army into the city of Orleans, which the English had almost captured. In her white, shining armor, this young heroine rode with her banner flying above her. On it were the names of JESUS and MARY. She was hit by an arrow in the great battle of Orleans, but she kept on urging her men to victory. At last they won! St. Joan and her army won more and more battles. The English armies had to retreat.

After the victories, Joan's time of suffering began. She was captured by the enemy. The ungrateful French king did not even try to save her. She was put in prison and after an unfair trial, was burned at the stake. Joan was not even twenty. She had a great horror of fire. Yet she went bravely to her death on May 29, 1431. Her last word was "Jesus." Four hundred and eighty-nine years later, on May 16, 1920, Pope Benedict XV proclaimed Joan a saint.

Joan was asked by God to accomplish a very difficult, nearly impossible, task. Joan was heroic. When we have to do something hard, we can ask St. Joan to help us.

❦

MAY 31

THE VISITATION OF MARY

Visitation means "visit." The Archangel Gabriel told the Blessed Virgin Mary that her cousin Elizabeth was going to have a baby. Elizabeth was an older woman. Mary knew that she might appreciate some help. She started out at once on the journey.

Mary's trip was long and dangerous. It was uncomfortable, too. But that could not stop her. She rode on a donkey. Mary reached her cousin's house. She was the first to greet Elizabeth. At that moment, God revealed to Elizabeth that Mary had become his mother. Elizabeth asked joyfully, "How have I deserved that the Mother of my Lord should come to me?" Mary remained humble. She quickly gave all the credit to God. He had blessed her so richly.

"My soul magnifies the Lord, and my spirit has rejoiced in God my Savior," she said. "For he has regarded the lowliness of his handmaid, and holy is his name."

What graces the Blessed Mother brought to the home of her cousin! St. John, while still hidden in his mother's womb, was cleansed of original sin. Zachary was able to speak again. St. Elizabeth was filled with the gifts of the Holy Spirit.

Mary stayed three months at her cousin's home. With great kindness and love, she helped Elizabeth.

Elizabeth's home was filled with grace through Mary's visit. We will be blessed, too, if we are devoted to our Heavenly Mother.

JUNE

ST. JUSTIN

St. Justin was from Samaria. He lived in the second century. His father brought him up without any belief in God. When he was a boy, Justin read poetry, history and science. As he grew up, he kept on studying. His main purpose for studying was to find the truth about God.

One day as he was walking along the shore of the sea, Justin met an old man. They began to talk together. Since Justin looked troubled, the man asked him what was on his mind. Justin answered that he was unhappy because he had not found anything certain about God in all the books he had read. The old man told him about Jesus, the Savior. He encouraged Justin to pray so that he would be able to understand the truth about God.

St. Justin began to pray and to read the Word of God, the Bible. He grew to love it very much. He was also impressed to see how brave the Christians were who were dying for their belief in and love for Jesus. After learning more about the Christian religion, Justin became a Christian. Then he used his great knowledge to explain and defend the faith with many writings.

It was in Rome that St. Justin was arrested for being a Christian. The judge asked him, "Do you think that by dying you will enter heaven and be rewarded?" "I don't just think so," the saint answered. "I am sure of it!" And he died a martyr around the year 166.

To keep our faith strong, we can pray an act of faith often. A very short act of faith we might repeat from time to time is: "My God, I believe in you."

❧

ST. MARCELLINUS AND ST. PETER

These two saints are mentioned in the First Eucharistic Prayer of the Mass. They were widely honored and prayed to by the early Christians. The feast of these two martyrs was included in the Roman calendar of saints by Pope Vigilius in 555.

Marcellinus was a priest and Peter assisted Marcellinus in his ministry. Both were very brave in the practice of their Christian faith. They served the Christian community with great self-sacrifice. During the persecution of Diocletian, many Christians were killed. These two men were among them. They were beheaded. It seems that before they died, however, they were forced to dig their own graves. They were taken to a hidden location to perform their difficult task. It was a forest called the Silva Nigra. Some time later, their graves were discovered in that remote spot. Their executioner eventually repented of the killings and became a

Christian. He led devout Christians to the remains, which were then buried in the catacomb of St. Tiberius. Pope Gregory IV sent the relics to Frankfurt, Germany, in 827. He believed that the relics of these two saints would bring blessings to the Church in that nation.

We can learn from martyrs that our lives have to become mirrors of our belief in Jesus. We can pray to St. Marcellinus and St. Peter and ask them for the grace to grow in our faith and love.

JUNE 3

ST. CHARLES LWANGA AND COMPANIONS

Christianity was still quite new to Uganda, Africa, when a Catholic mission was started in 1879. The priests were members of the Missionaries of Africa. Because of their white religious habit, they became popularly known as the "White Fathers." King Mwanga did not know what Christianity was all about. But he became angry when a Catholic, Joseph Mkasa, corrected him for the way he was living. The king had murdered a group of Christians and their Anglican bishop. The king was also involved in homosexual activity. He was especially interested in his court pages. King Mwanga's anger turned into resentment and hatred for Joseph Mkasa and his religion. A few of the king's ambitious officers fueled his fears with lies. Joseph Mkasa was beheaded on November 18, 1885. The persecution had begun. Before it was over, a hundred people died. Twenty-two of them would be declared saints.

With the death of Joseph Mkasa, Charles Lwanga became the chief religion teacher of the king's Catholic pages. On May 26, 1886, the king found out that some of his pages were Catholic. He called in Denis Sebuggwawo. He asked Denis if he had been teaching religion to another page. Denis said yes. The king grabbed his spear and flung it violently through the young man's throat. Then the king shouted that no one was permitted to leave his headquarters. War drums beat throughout the night. In a hidden room, Charles Lwanga secretly baptized four pages. One was St. Kizito, a cheerful, generous thirteen-year-old. He was the youngest of the group. St. Charles Lwanga had often protected Kizito from the king's lust.

Most of the twenty-two Uganda martyrs who have been proclaimed saints were killed on June 3, 1886. They were forced to walk thirty-seven miles to the execution site. After a few days in prison, they were thrown into a huge fire. Seventeen of the martyrs were royal pages. One of the martyred boys was St. Mbaga. His own father was the executioner that day. Another of the martyrs, St. Andrew Kagwa, died on January 27, 1887. He was among the twenty-two proclaimed saints in 1964 by Pope Paul VI.

St. Charles Lwanga is the patron of black African young people. He and his companions greatly appreciated their gift of faith. They were heroes! We all can pray to St. Charles and these African martyrs. We can ask them to show us how to witness to Jesus and the Church as they did.

❧

ST. FRANCIS CARACCIOLO

Francis was born in the Abruzzi region of Italy on October 13, 1563. His father was a Neapolitan prince. His mother claimed relationship to the Aquino family among whom was the thirteenth-century saint, Thomas Aquinas. Francis had a good upbringing. He was active in sports. Then, when he was twenty-two, a disease, something like leprosy, brought him close to death. While he was sick, he thought about the emptiness of the pleasures of the world. He realized that real happiness could only be found in something deeper. Francis made a vow that if he got better, he would dedicate his life to God. The disease left him so fast that it seemed like a miracle. Francis kept his promise. He began his studies to become a priest.

Later, as a newly ordained priest, Father Francis joined a group who were devoted to prison ministry. They cared for the prisoners and prepared condemned men to die a good death. He and another priest, John Augustine Adorno, started a religious congregation. When Father Adorno died, Francis was chosen superior. He was not comfortable at all with this position. So humble was he that he actually signed his letters, "Francis the sinner." He also took his turn, along with the other priests, sweeping the floors, making beds and washing dishes.

Father Francis often spent almost the whole night praying in church. He wanted all the priests to spend at least one hour a day in prayer before the Blessed Sacrament. St. Francis spoke so often and so well about God's love for us that he became known as "the preacher of the love of God."

St. Francis did not live a long life. He died in 1607 at the age of forty-four. Just before he died, he suddenly cried, "Let's go!" "Where do you want to go?" asked the priest by his bed. "To heaven! To heaven!" came the answer in a clear, happy voice. Soon after, he died. He was proclaimed a saint by Pope Pius VII in 1807.

In his second letter to the Corinthians, St. Paul reminds us that "God loves the cheerful giver." This was the kind of person St. Francis Caracciolo was. If we need a little help in becoming more generous with our time and energy, we can ask this saint to help us. We can ask him also to make us the cheerful givers that Paul describes.

ST. BONIFACE

This great apostle of Germany was born in Wessex, England, between the years 672 and 680. When he was small, some missionaries stayed a while at his home. They told the boy all about their work. They were so happy and excited about bringing the Good News to people. Boniface decided in his heart that he would be just like them when he grew up. While still young, he went to a monastery school to be educated. Some years later, he became a popular teacher. When he was ordained a priest, he was a powerful preacher because he was so full of enthusiasm.

Boniface wanted everyone to have the opportunity to know about and love Jesus and his Church. He became a missionary to the western part of Germany. Pope St. Gregory II blessed him and sent him on this mission. Boniface preached with great success. He was gentle and kind. He was also a man of great courage. Once, to prove that the pagan gods were false, he did a bold thing. There was a certain huge oak tree called the "oak of Thor." The pagans believed it was sacred to their gods. In front of a large crowd, Boniface struck the tree a few times with an axe. The big tree crashed. The pagans realized that their gods were false when nothing happened to Boniface.

Everywhere he preached, new members were received into the Church. In his lifetime, Boniface converted great numbers of people. In place of the statues of the pagan gods, he built churches and monasteries. In 732, the new pope, St. Gregory III made Boniface an archbishop and gave him another mission territory. It was Bavaria, which is part of Germany today. He and some companions went there to teach the people about the true faith. Here, too, the holy bishop was very successful.

Then, one day, he was preparing to confirm some converts. A group of fierce warriors swooped down on the camp. Boniface would not let his companions defend him. "Our Lord tells us to repay evil with good," he said. "The day has come for which I have waited so long. Trust in God and he will save us." The Barbarians attacked, and Boniface was the first one killed. He died a martyr on June 5, 754. He was buried at the famous monastery he had started at Fulda, Germany. This was what he wanted.

Still today large numbers of people do not know the true God. We can pray for them. If God inspires us to become missionaries, we can ask St. Boniface to help us follow the call.

JUNE 6

ST. NORBERT

Norbert was born in Germany around the year 1080. He was good while a child and teenager. Then at the court of Emperor Henry V, Norbert spent all his time on frivolous things. He thought only of acquiring positions of honor. He was the first to arrive at parties and celebrations. He was thoroughly happy with "the good life." One day, however, he was frightened by a flash of lightning. His horse bolted. Norbert was thrown to the ground and knocked unconscious. When he woke, he began to think seriously about the way his life was going. God felt very near. Norbert realized that the Lord was offering him the grace to change for the better. Gradually, he went back to the idea he had once had several years earlier. He had considered becoming a priest. Now he would. He was ordained to the priesthood in 1115.

Father Norbert worked hard to make others turn from their worldly ways. He gave a good example by selling all he had to give the money to the poor. St. Norbert became the founder of a congregation for the spreading of the faith. His original group began their religious life as a community of thirteen. They lived in the valley of Premontre. That is why they are called Premonstratensians.They are also called Norbertines, after their founder.

St. Norbert was chosen bishop of the city of Magdeburg. He entered the city wearing very poor clothes and no shoes. The porter at the door of the bishop's house did not know him and refused to let him in. He told him to go join the other beggars. "But he is our new bishop!" shouted those who knew the saint. The porter was shocked and very sorry. "Never mind, dear brother," St. Norbert said kindly. "You judge me more correctly than those who brought me here."

St. Norbert had to combat a heresy which denied that Jesus is really present in the Holy Eucharist. His beautiful words about Our Lord's presence in the Blessed Sacrament brought the people back to their holy faith. In March, 1133, he and his great friend, St. Bernard (whose feast is celebrated on August 20) walked in an unusual procession. They joined the emperor and his army to accompany the true pope, Innocent II, safely to the Vatican.

St. Norbert died in 1134. Pope Gregory XIII proclaimed him a saint in 1582.

We can learn many good things from St. Norbert, especially to take life seriously. We can also learn to appreciate Jesus in the Holy Eucharist and receive him with faith and love.

JUNE 7

BLESSED ANNE
OF ST. BARTHOLOMEW

Anne was the daughter of peasants. She took care of sheep until she was twenty. Four miles from her hometown was Avila, the city where St. Teresa and her Carmelite nuns lived. Anne was accepted into the order. She became a lay sister rather than a cloistered nun. Sister Anne could go out on errands and do what was necessary to take care of the community.

For the last seven years of her life, St. Teresa chose this sister, Blessed Anne, to be her traveling companion. St. Teresa went around to visit the communities of nuns. Sometimes she started a new convent. Sometimes she helped the nuns become more enthusiastic about the wonderful life they had chosen. St. Teresa thought very highly of Blessed Anne and praised her to the other nuns.

Although Blessed Anne did not have the opportunity to go to school, she knew how to read and write. She recorded her adventures with the great St. Teresa. It was Blessed Anne who was with her when she died.

Blessed Anne's life continued quite normally for six years after St. Teresa's death. Then the superiors decided to open a new convent in Paris, France. Five nuns were selected to go and Blessed

Anne was one of them. While the people of Paris were warmly greeting the nuns, Blessed Anne slipped into the kitchen and prepared a meal for the hungry community. Eventually, four of the five nuns moved on to the Netherlands. Anne remained behind because she had been appointed the prioress. It seems that she reminded the Lord that most of the young French women joining their community were from rich, noble families. She explained to him that she was only a shepherd. Within her heart, Blessed Anne heard the Lord's answer: "With straws I light my fire."

Anne was sent to the Netherlands to start more new convents. She went first to Mons and then to Antwerp. The young women who came to join the Carmelites thought of Anne as a saint. Anne died in Antwerp in 1626. She was proclaimed "blessed" by Pope Benedict XV.

Blessed Anne loved to be in the background. She was not ambitious. Whenever we find ourselves wanting to be important, we can pray to this holy nun. She will help us concentrate on impressing God rather than people.

JUNE 8

ST. WILLIAM OF YORK

William Fitzherbert was born in England in the twelfth century. He was the nephew of King Stephen. As a young man, William was rather easy-going and even a bit lazy. He seems to have given the impression to some that he was not very serious about taking responsibility in life. However, William was very popular with the people of his city of York.

Years later, when the archbishop of York died, William was chosen to take his place. In those times, princes used to interfere in the election of the bishops. This is why many priests did not think William had been properly chosen. It was his uncle, the king, who had appointed him. Even the great St. Bernard persuaded the pope to make someone else archbishop of York. William was asked to step aside because they felt his appointment was not valid. He left his bishop's house feeling hurt and humiliated. He went to live with another uncle, a bishop. It seems that William became a much more spiritual person. He would not accept any of the comforts his uncle offered him. He prayed and performed penances. He began to show how much he cared about his faith and about the Church.

The people of York were angry at what had happened to their archbishop. They could not understand how something like this could take place. There were street fights between those who wanted William and those who did not. Six years passed. William lived a quiet life of prayer in the home of his uncle, the bishop. He asked the Lord for peace for his archdiocese. It did not matter any more if he had been treated unjustly. What mattered was that his people be taken care of.

Finally, his prayers were answered. When the other archbishop died, the pope sent William back to York. He arrived in May, 1154. The people were very happy. But William was an old man by this time, and about a month later, he died. He was proclaimed a saint by Pope Honorius III in 1227.

Sometimes people say things about us that are untrue or exaggerated. We can ask St. William to help us be as forgiving as he was. We can ask him also to show us how to move on with our lives and not to waste time thinking about our hurts.

JUNE 9

ST. EPHREM

Ephrem was born in Mesopotamia around the year 306. He was baptized when he was eighteen. Ephrem eventually went into the hills and became a hermit. He found a cave near the city of Edessa in Syria. His clothes were just patched rags and he ate what the earth provided.

Ephrem became angry easily. He gradually gained control over himself. People who met him thought he was just naturally very calm. He often went to preach in Edessa. When he spoke about God's judgment, the people wept. He would tell them that he was a great sinner. He really meant it, too, because although his sins were small, they seemed very big to him. When St. Basil met him, he asked, "Are you Ephrem, the famous servant of Jesus?" Ephrem answered quickly, "I am Ephrem who walks unworthily on the way to salvation." Then he asked and received advice from St. Basil on how to grow in the spiritual life.

Ephrem spent his time writing spiritual books. He wrote in several languages—Syriac, Greek, Latin and Armenian. These works are so beautiful and spiritual that they have been translated into many languages. They are still read today. Ephrem also wrote hymns for public worship. These hymns became very popular. As the people sang them, they learned much about the faith. That is why he is called "the harp of the Holy Spirit." Because he was such a great teacher through his writings, in 1920 he was proclaimed a Doctor of the Church.

Ephrem died in June, 373.

One way to praise God at the Eucharist is to join in the singing of the hymns. This is what Ephrem would do if he were kneeling next to us at Mass.

JUNE 10

BLESSED HENRY OF TREVISO

Henry was born in Bolzano, Italy. He lived during the last part of the thirteenth and early part of the fourteenth centuries. Henry's family was very poor, so he had no opportunity to learn to read and write. When he was a teenager, he moved to Treviso to find work. He became a day laborer. Few people realized that he gave away most of his earnings to the poor. He went to Mass daily and received communion as often as was permitted. Henry loved the sacrament of Reconciliation, too, and found this sacrament of a forgiving God very encouraging.

People began to notice the kind of Christian Henry was. He made it his penance to be very diligent at his job. And he allowed ample time every day for private prayer, usually at church. Henry was known for his calm and gentle ways. Sometimes people teased him because he seemed like such a simple person. As he grew older, he began to look shabby and stooped. Children would comment at times on his peculiar appearance. But Henry didn't mind. He realized that they did not know they were hurting him.

When Henry was too old and frail to work, a friend James Castagnolis, brought him into his own home. Mr. Castagnolis gave Henry a room, and food when the old man would accept it.

Blessed Henry insisted that he live on the alms of the people of Treviso. They were generous in their donations of food because they knew he shared their gifts with many people who were poor and homeless. By the end of his life, Henry could barely walk. People watched with awe as the old man dragged himself to morning Mass. Often he would visit other local churches as well, painfully moving toward each destination.

What a mystery this good man was. When he died on June 10, 1315, people crowded into his little room. They wanted a relic, a keepsake. They found his treasures: a prickly hair-shirt, a log of wood that was his pillow, some straw that was the mattress for his bed. His body was moved to the cathedral so that all the people could pay their tribute. Over two hundred miracles were reported within a few days after his death.

Henry of Treviso was declared "blessed" by Pope Benedict XIV.

Blessed Henry teaches us that we don't have to do great things to become holy. We can ask him to show us how to live fervent Christian lives daily.

JUNE 11

ST. BARNABAS

Although not one of the original twelve apostles, Barnabas is called an apostle by St. Luke in his Acts of the Apostles. This is because, like Paul the apostle, Barnabas received a special mission from God. He was a Jew born on the island of Cyprus. His name was Joseph, but the apostles changed it to Barnabas. This name means "son of consolation."

As soon as he became a Christian, St. Barnabas sold all he owned and gave the money to the apostles. He was a good, kind-hearted man. He was full of enthusiasm to share his belief in and love for Jesus. He was sent to the city of Antioch to preach the Gospel. Antioch was the third largest city in the Roman Empire. Here is where the followers of Jesus were first called Christians. Barnabas realized that he needed help. He thought of Paul of Tarsus. He believed that Paul's conversion had been real. It was Barnabas who convinced St. Peter and the Christian community. He asked Paul to come and work with him. Barnabas was a humble person, and was not afraid of sharing the responsibility and the power. He knew that Paul, too, had a great gift to give and he wanted him to have the chance.

Sometime later, the Holy Spirit chose Paul and Barnabas for a special assignment. Not long afterward, the two apostles set off on a daring missionary journey. They had many sufferings to bear and often risked their lives. Despite the hardships, their preaching won many people to Jesus and his Church.

Later St. Barnabas went on another missionary journey, this time with his relative, John Mark. They went to Barnabas' own country of Cyprus. So many people became believers through his preaching that Barnabas is called the apostle of Cyprus. It is commonly believed that this great saint was stoned to death in the year 61.

Barnabas received a name that symbolized what he was—a good person who encouraged others to love the Lord, too. We can pray to this saint to ask him to make us sons and daughters of "consolation" as he was.

JUNE 12

ST. JOHN OF SAHAGUN

St. John was born at Sahagun, Spain, in the fifteenth century. He received his education from the Benedictine monks of his town. Then John became a parish priest. He could have lived a very comfortable life in the cathedral parish or in other wealthy parishes. However, John felt attracted to the poverty and simple lifestyle that Jesus had lived. Father John chose to keep charge only of a small chapel. There he celebrated Mass, preached and taught catechism.

Father John realized that he needed to know theology better. He enrolled in classes at the great Catholic University of Salamanca. After four years of hard study, he became famous as a preacher. Nine years later, he joined a community of Augustinian friars. They were very impressed by the way he practiced the Christian virtues. He was obedient to his superiors and humble, too. He also continued his preaching. His beautiful homilies or sermons brought about a change in the people of Salamanca. They had been quarreling violently among themselves. Often young noblemen fought each other in revenge. St. John succeeded in ending many of these bitter fights. He even persuaded people to forgive one another.

He was not afraid to correct evils, even when the evildoers were powerful people who could take revenge. Once he corrected a duke for the way he was making the poor people suffer. What the priest said was true! In anger, the duke sent two of his men to kill St. John. The two men found the priest and approached him. Father John was so calm and kind. Both men were overcome with sorrow and asked his pardon. Then the duke became sick. Through the prayers of St. John, he repented of his sins and recovered.

It was the graces he received from prayer and from the Mass that gave St. John his special power as a preacher. He celebrated the Mass with great devotion.

St. John of Sahagun died on June 11, 1479. He was proclaimed a saint by Pope Alexander VIII in 1690.

We will be so much more effective Christians if we can be calm and peaceful in our whole manner of speaking and acting. We will never spread the Good News if we are overbearing and rude. We can ask St. John of Sahagun to show us how to be as peace-loving and kind as he was.

JUNE 13

ST. ANTHONY OF PADUA

This very popular saint was born in Portugal in 1195. He was baptized "Ferdinand." He received an excellent education from the Augustinian friars and joined the order. When he was twenty-five, his life took an exciting turn. He heard about some Franciscans who had been martyred by the Moors in Morocco. These friars were St. Berard and companions. We celebrate their feast on January 16. From then on, Ferdinand felt a strong desire to die for Christ. He joined the Franciscans. This order was very new. St. Francis himself was still alive. Ferdinand took the name "Anthony." He went off to Africa to preach to the Moors. But he soon became so sick that he had to return to Italy.

No one in his new religious order realized how brilliant and talented he was. They were not aware of how much education he had received. He never spoke about himself. So the Franciscan superiors assigned him to a quiet friary in Italy. There he

washed pots and pans. One day, at a large gathering of priests, Anthony preached a marvelous sermon. From then on, until he died nine years later, St. Anthony preached all over Italy. He was so popular that people even closed their stores to go to hear him.

St. Anthony is frequently called on in times of physical as well as spiritual needs. Many miracles have taken place through the intercession of St. Anthony. Large numbers of people have obtained favors by praying to him. That is why he is called the "wonder-worker." The statue of St. Anthony shows him with Baby Jesus because Baby Jesus appeared to him. Other pictures show St. Anthony holding a bible. This is because he knew, loved and preached the Word of God so well. In fact, St. Anthony was so well educated especially in Sacred Scripture that Pope Pius XII proclaimed him the "Evangelical Doctor," or Doctor of Sacred Scripture.

St. Anthony died at Arcella, near Padua, Italy, on June 13, 1231. He was thirty-six. He was proclaimed a saint by Pope Gregory IX one year later.

Sometimes we want to be recognized for the good things we do or know how to do. It could be that we won't always receive much attention. That is when we can ask St. Anthony to teach us how to be satisfied. We can ask him to help us concentrate on what we can give in this life, not just what we can get.

JUNE 14

ST. METHODIUS I

St. Methodius lived in the ninth century. He was born and raised in Sicily. Methodius had received an excellent education and he wanted a position worthy of it. He decided to sail to Constantinople to seek an important job at the emperor's court. Somewhere in his travels, he met a holy monk who shared with him long, deep conversations. All of the questions about God and eternity came to Methodius' mind. The monk helped him see that to find real joy in life he should give himself to God in religious life. So when Methodius arrived in Constantinople, he passed up the palace and went to a monastery instead.

The Christians were having serious difficulties in Constantinople. Some felt that it was wrong to have religious pictures and icons. They mistakenly thought that people were praying to the picture or statue, not to the person it represented. There were bitter fights and the emperor was involved. He agreed with the people who thought that pictures and statues were evil. St. Methodius, on the other hand, did not agree with the emperor. He understood why Christians needed pictures and statues. He was chosen to go to Rome and ask the pope to straighten out the situation. When he returned, the emperor punished him with a prison term of seven years. Methodius suffered in a dark, damp prison but he wouldn't let his spirit be crushed. He knew that Jesus would use his sufferings to help the Church. Finally, in 842 the emperor died. His wife, Theodora, ruled because her son was a baby. Theodora had a different opinion than her husband, the emperor had. She felt that people should be free to have statues, icons and sacred pictures if they wanted them. Methodius and those who had suffered for a long time were so happy. Now they were free.

One of the people who had made St. Methodius suffer the most was sent into exile by the empress. Then Methodius became the patriarch of Constantinople. The people loved him very much.

St. Methodius wrote beautiful essays about theology and the spiritual life. He also wrote lives of saints and poetry.

Four years after becoming patriarch, Methodius died. It was June 14, 847.

St. Methodius started out his career looking for positions and wealth. Then, he listened to a holy monk and chose a much harder life. When we are offered choices even in smaller things, we can say a little prayer to St. Methodius. He will give us the wisdom to choose what is the best for us for this life and for our life in eternity with God.

JUNE 15

ST. GERMAINE OF PIBRAC

Pibrac is the little village in France where Germaine was born around 1579. She spent her life there. She was always a sickly girl and not pretty. In fact, her right hand was deformed and helpless. Her father paid little attention to her. Her stepmother did not want her around her own healthy children. So Germaine slept with the sheep in the barn, even in cold weather. She dressed in rags and was laughed at by other children. She spent all day tending the sheep out in the fields. When she came home at night, her stepmother often screamed at her and beat her.

Yet this poor girl learned to talk with God and to remember that he was with her all the time. She always managed to get to daily Mass. She left her sheep in care of her guardian angel. Never once did one wander away from her shepherd's staff she planted in the ground.

Germaine often gathered young children around her to teach them about the faith. She wanted their hearts to be full of God's love. She tried her best to help the poor, too. She shared with beggars the little bit of food she was given to eat. One winter day, her stepmother accused her of stealing bread. The woman chased her with a stick. But what fell from Germaine's apron was not bread. It was summer flowers.

By now people no longer made fun of Germaine. In fact, they loved and admired her. She could have begun to live in her father's house, but she chose to keep on sleeping in the barn. Then, one morning in 1601, when she was twenty-two, she was found dead on her straw mattress. Her life of great suffering was over. God worked miracles to show that she was a saint.

The main virtue of this saint was patience. She carried her big cross well, because she received Holy Communion often. In our little sufferings, let us turn to Our Lord in Holy Communion and ask his help.

JUNE 16

ST. JOHN FRANCIS REGIS

This French saint was born in 1597. When he was eighteen, he entered the Jesuit order. In the seminary, John's love for God and his vocation showed in the way he prayed. He was also eager to teach catechism in the parishes when he could. After he was ordained a priest, St. John Francis began his work as a missionary preacher. He gave very simple talks that came right from his heart. He especially spoke to the poor, ordinary folks. They came in great crowds to hear him. He spent his mornings praying, performing the sacrament of Reconciliation and preaching. In the afternoon, he would visit prisons and hospitals. To someone who said that the prisoners and bad women he converted would not stay good for long, the saint answered: "If my efforts stop just one sin from being committed, I shall consider them worthwhile."

St. John Francis journeyed to wild mountain parishes even on the coldest days of winter to preach his missions. "I have seen him stand all day on a heap of snow at the top of a mountain preaching," one priest said, "and then spend the whole night hearing confessions." Sometimes he would start off for a far-away town at three o'clock in the morning with a few apples in his pocket for his day's food.

Once, on his way to a village, St. John Francis fell and broke his leg. But he kept on going, leaning on a stick and on his companion's shoulder. When he reached the village, he went at once to hear confessions. He did not have his leg taken care of. At the end of the day, when the doctor looked at it, his leg was already completely healed.

St. John Francis died on one of his preaching missions. He became very ill while lost at night in the woods. Just before he died, he exclaimed: "I see Our Lord and his mother opening heaven for me." He died on December 31, 1640.

In 1806, a pilgrim joined the crowds going to pray at the shrine of St. John Francis Regis. The pilgrim believed all his life that this saint obtained his vocation to the priesthood. That man was St. John Vianney, the Cure of Ars. His feast is celebrated on August 4.

The life of St. John Francis reminds us that God has many blessings and graces for us if we are willing to forget our own wants sometimes. This way we can help our parents, family and friends in their needs.

JUNE 17

ST. EMILY DE VIALAR

Emily de Vialar was an only child. She was born in France in 1797. Her wealthy parents sent her to school in Paris. She returned to her small town of Gaillac when her mother died. Fifteen-year-old Emily would be good company for her father. Mr. de Vialar was interested in finding a suitable husband for his daughter. He became angry when Emily flatly refused to marry. He started arguments frequently and shouted his frustrations at her. Emily knew that she wanted to be a religious sister and give her life to God.

When Emily was twenty-one, a new priest arrived in Gaillac. His name was Father Mercier. He directed Emily in her vocation. She wanted to help the poor and the sick. Father Mercier helped her set up an out-patient service right on the terrace of the de Vialar home. Emily's father was upset by all the bother. This tense situation between Emily and her father existed for fifteen years. Then Emily's grandfather, the Baron de Portal, died. He left her a fortune and at last she could have the independence she needed to begin her great work for God.

With the help of Father Mercier, Emily bought a large house in her hometown. She and three other women began a religious order. They designed a habit and chose a name. They called themselves the Sisters of St. Joseph of the Apparition. (In Matthew's Gospel, an angel had appeared to Joseph to tell him that Mary's child was from God.) The archbishop blessed their congregation and ministry. These sisters would be dedicated to the care of the sick and poor, and to the education of children. Twelve young women joined the group within three months. Sister Emily pronounced her vows in 1835 along with seventeen other sisters. The archbishop approved the rule of the sisters.

The Sisters of St. Joseph started branch convents. In 1847, the sisters went to Burma and in 1854, to Australia. In forty years, Mother Emily saw her congregation grow from the patio of her home in Gaillac, France, to some forty foundations around the world.

Mother Emily wrote many letters which revealed her tremendous love for God, for his Church and for people. She cared about everybody. She saw in her heart people everywhere who needed the truth of the Gospel and the love that Christianity brings. She asked Jesus for the strength she needed to continue on. Mother Emily's health began to fail around 1850. She died on August 24, 1856. Pope Pius XII proclaimed her a saint in 1951.

Instead of quitting when things get hard, we can ask St. Emily de Vialar to make us strong and patient as she was.

BLESSED GREGORY BARBARIGO

Blessed Gregory was born in 1625. He was raised and educated in his native city of Venice, Italy. While still in his twenties, he was chosen by the officials of Venice to represent them in Munster, Germany, at an important event. Leaders were meeting to sign the Treaty of Westphalia on October 24, 1648. This treaty would bring to an end the Thirty Year War. This war, begun in 1618, was fought in Germany. It involved local, Swedish and French troops and was basically caused by Catholic-Protestant misunderstanding.

At Munster, Blessed Gregory met the pope's representative. This man was to become Pope Alexander VII in 1655. He realized the goodness and spiritual qualities of Father Gregory. He made him a bishop and assigned him to the diocese of Bergamo, Italy. In 1660, the pope called him to Rome again. This time he made Blessed Gregory a cardinal and assigned him to Padua.

Blessed Gregory was to spend the rest of his life in that city already made famous by St. Anthony. People often said that Cardinal Barbarigo was like a second Cardinal Borromeo. We celebrate the feast of St. Charles Borromeo on November 4.

Cardinal Barbarigo lived a plain, self-sacrificing life. He gave large sums of money for charitable needs. He kept his door open and was always available when people were in trouble. He started an excellent college and seminary for the training of men to be priests. He gave the seminary a first-rate library with many books by the early Church fathers and books about Sacred Scripture. He even equipped the seminary with a printing press.

Blessed Gregory Barbarigo died on June 15, 1697, at the age of seventy-two. He was proclaimed "blessed" in 1761 by Pope Clement XIII.

When we pray, it is a good idea to ask the Lord for the grace to know and recognize his plan for our lives. When we find something hard or tiresome, we might want to spend time thinking about the way Blessed Gregory Barbarigo used his time. He became a generous, loving person who brought many people closer to God by his good example.

JUNE 19

ST. ROMUALD

Romuald, an Italian nobleman, was born around 951 in Ravenna, Italy. When he was twenty, he was shocked to see his father kill a man in a duel. Romuald went to a Benedictine monastery. He wanted to set his own life straight. He also wanted to do penance for his father's drastic deed. The monastery surroundings and lifestyle were new to Romuald. He was used to luxury and laziness until then. The nobleman was impressed by the good example of many of the monks. He decided to become a monk. He asked a good hermit named Marinus to teach him how to become holy. Both Marinus and Romuald tried to spend each day praising and loving God. Romuald's own father Sergius came to observe his son's new way of life. The man was struck by the simplicity and spirit of self-sacrifice. Sergius realized that there had to be great happiness in the monastery because his son freely chose to stay there. That was all Sergius needed. He gave up his wealth and followed his son to spend the rest of his life as a monk too.

Eventually, Romuald began the Camaldolese Benedictine order. He traveled around Italy starting hermitages and monasteries. Wherever he went, he gave his monks a wonderful example of penance. For a whole year, all he ate each day was a bit of boiled beans. Then for three years, he ate only the little food he grew himself. Through these sacrifices Romuald grew closer to God.

Romuald died on June 19, 1027, at the monastery of Valdi-Castro. He was alone in his cell and passed away quietly, no doubt whispering his favorite prayer: "Oh, my sweet Jesus! God of my heart! Delight of pure souls! The object of all my desires!"

Let us ask St. Romuald to help us value prayer and the life of Jesus within us. We can also ask Romuald to obtain for us the grace to keep our priorities straight. He knows how challenging that can be.

JUNE 20

BLESSED MICHELINA

Michelina was born in 1300, in Pesaro, Italy. Her family was wealthy and she married a rich man. Michelina was a happy person by nature. She seemed always like she did not have a problem in the world. But when she was just twenty, her husband died. All of a sudden, Michelina found herself alone with a little son to raise.

The young mother seemed anxious to find happiness in the things around her. Her life became a stream of parties and fun and fancy meals. She couldn't seem to have enough of the good things that life offered. After a while, she realized that she had to be with her child more. She also had to be accountable for how she used her money and time. She felt so empty inside. Michelina finally settled down and became a responsible adult.

A holy Franciscan lay woman lived in Pesaro. Her name was Syriaca. Syriaca realized that Michelina was really a wonderful person who needed direction and help to be more spiritual. Syriaca and Michelina became friends and the holy woman greatly influenced her. Michelina became prayerful. She took care of her child and home with diligence. She spent her free time serving the poor and needy. She visited the lonely and took care of those too sick or too old to look after themselves. Eventually, she became a lay Franciscan. At first, her relatives were concerned when she gave away her fancy clothes and started to eat plain food. But after a while, they became convinced that Michelina was truly a spiritual woman.

Michelina lived her whole life in the same house in Pesaro. She died in 1356 at the age of fifty-six. In her memory, the people of her town kept a lamp always lit in her home. In 1590, Blessed Michelina's house was made into a church.

Michelina had the choice to live a selfish, easy life or to be a self-sacrificing and loving Christian. It was through the example of Syriaca that Michelina became holy. We can ask Blessed Michelina to help us have the courage to imitate people we know who are good examples.

❦

JUNE 21

ST. ALOYSIUS GONZAGA

Aloysius, the patron of Catholic youth, was born on March 9, 1568. Since he was so full of life, his father planned to make a great soldier out of him. When Aloysius was just five, his father took him to the army camp. There little Aloysius marched in parade. He even managed to load and fire a gun one day while the army was at rest. He learned rough language from the soldiers, too.

When he found out what the words meant, he felt very bad that he used them.

As he grew, Aloysius was sent to the courts of dukes and princes. Dishonesty, hatred and impurity were common. But the only effect it all had on St. Aloysius was to make him more careful to live his own Christian commitment. He became sick. That gave him an excuse to spend some time praying and reading good books. When Aloysius was sixteen, he decided to become a Jesuit priest. His father refused his consent. However, after three years, he finally gave in. Once Aloysius had joined the order, he asked to do hard and humble tasks. He served in the kitchen and washed the dishes. He used to say, "I am a crooked piece of iron. I came to religion to be made straight by the hammer of mortification and penance."

When the plague broke out in Rome, Aloysius asked to be allowed to care for the sick. He who had always had servants to wait on him gladly washed the sick and made their beds. He served them until he caught the sickness himself.

St. Aloysius was only twenty-three when he died. It was the night of June 20, 1591. He said simply, "I am going to heaven." The body of St. Aloysius Gonzaga is buried in the Church of St. Ignatius in Rome. He was proclaimed a saint by Pope Benedict XIII in 1726.

If we know that peer pressure can make us say and do things we shouldn't, we can ask St. Aloysius for the courage to do what is right.

❧

ST. PAULINUS OF NOLA

St. Paulinus was born around 353 in Bordeaux,
France. His father was a governor and a wealthy
landowner. Paulinus received a good education.
He became a lawyer and poet. He traveled in
France, Spain and Italy, wherever work or plea-
sure took him. In 381, at the age of twenty-eight, he
became the governor of Campania, Italy.

When he was thirty-six, Paulinus became a
Catholic. He and his wife, Theresia, had one child,
a son. After their son died, the couple gave away
their wealth and property to the poor. They kept
only what they needed to live on. Paulinus and
Theresia agreed that they wanted to live simply.
The couple prayed, made sacrifices and did without unnecessary things. They also chose to take a
vow of chastity to witness to their love for Jesus.
Paulinus and his wife were greatly admired by the
Christian community. They were very pleased
when Paulinus became a priest in 394. Then he and
Theresia started a small community of monks in
Nola, Italy. They opened a hospice for poor people
and travelers, too.

Paulinus and Theresia decided to remain in Nola. Paulinus wanted to be near the shrine of one of his favorite saints, St. Felix of Nola. St. Felix had been a priest and bishop who had died in 260. He had been a defender of his people during the cruel persecution by Emperor Decius. Bishop Felix had been known for his prayerfulness, his love for the people, and his poor lifestyle. Over a century later, Paulinus prayed to him and wrote about him. He felt great confidence in the power of St. Felix. What could this former Roman governor have in common with St. Felix? More than St. Paulinus could have guessed. In 409, he was chosen to be bishop of Nola. The people were so happy. He was a wise, gentle bishop, just as St. Felix had been. He was praised by many great saints who lived at that time, St. Ambrose, St. Augustine, St. Jerome, St. Martin of Tours and others. Although some of his wonderful writings have been lost, thirty-two poems and fifty-one letters remain.

St. Paulinus was bishop of Nola until his death in 431.

St. Paulinus became such a wonderful Catholic because he was full of appreciation for the gift of his faith. We can pray to St. Paulinus and ask him to lead us to grow in our gratefulness for the faith.

ST. JOHN FISHER

John Fisher was born in Yorkshire, England, in 1469. He was educated at Cambridge University and became a priest. Father Fisher taught at Cambridge, too. He was a wonderful teacher and helped the students grow in their knowledge of the faith. He was a theologian. Father Fisher was especially helpful in pointing out religious errors of the times that confused some people.

In 1504, he became the bishop of Rochester, England. It was a poor diocese and Bishop Fisher was to remain its shepherd for thirty years. So, Bishop Fisher performed two important duties. He was a bishop of a diocese and the head of Cambridge University. In 1514, he was appointed the head of the university for life. Bishop Fisher was also the priest who heard the confessions of King Henry VIII's mother. Her name was Elizabeth of York.

Bishop Fisher had many friends, including the famous scholar, Erasmus, and the great St. Thomas More. Little did Bishop Fisher and Thomas More know that they would be sharing a feast day on the calendar of saints.

It certainly was not a celebration when Bishop Fisher was put in prison in 1533. He was arrested for insisting that the marriage of the king and Queen Catherine was true. Then Henry VIII divorced Catherine and married Anne Boleyn in a civil ceremony. He demanded that people sign an oath of loyalty to him. He made himself the head of the Church in England. Bishop Fisher would not sign the oath. He was sent to the Tower of London. The tower was damp and the treatment was harsh. Bishop Fisher suffered very much, but he would not betray his faith. Even though there were no televisions and radios, people found out about what Bishop Fisher, Sir Thomas More and the others were going through. They were shocked and saddened. On June 12, 1535, Pope Paul III named Bishop Fisher a cardinal. He hoped this would make Henry free him. But the king only became more angry and mean. He demanded Cardinal Fisher's death. John Fisher was killed on June 22, 1535.

Along with his friend, St. Thomas More, Cardinal John Fisher was proclaimed a saint by Pope Pius XI in 1935.

Sometimes it's much easier to go along with the crowd rather than stand up for what is right. When you find yourself in a situation like that, pray to St. John Fisher for some of his courage.

ST. THOMAS MORE

Thomas More was a famous lawyer and writer. He was born in London in 1477. His father had been a lawyer, too, and a judge. Thomas was always grateful to his father for being so loving and for not spoiling him.

Thomas' first wife, Jane Colt, died very young. More was left with four small children. He was married again, to a widow, a simple woman who could not even read or write. Her husband tried to teach her. Thomas made home life enjoyable for his family because he was so pleasant to be with. During meals, one of the children would read from the Bible. Then they would have fun and tell jokes. St. Thomas often asked poorer neighbors in to dinner, too. He always helped the poor as much as he could. He loved to delight his guests with surprises. He even kept some playful monkeys as pets. Yet few could have imagined how deeply spiritual St. Thomas really was. He prayed long hours into the night and performed penances, too. He was very much aware that being a true Christian took the grace and help of God.

Thomas held important government positions. For three years he was lord chancellor, another name for prime minister. Henry VIII used to put his arm affectionately around Thomas' shoulder. Yet although the saint was a most loyal subject, he was loyal to God first of all. In fact, when the king

tried to make him disobey God's law, Thomas refused. Henry wanted to obtain a divorce from his wife to marry another woman. However, the pope could not give permission, since that is against God's law. Henry was stubborn and at last he left the Church. He wanted everyone to recognize him as the head of the Church in England. Thomas could not do that. He chose to remain faithful to the Catholic faith and to God. He was condemned to death for that, yet he forgave his judges. He even said he hoped he would see them in heaven. He really meant it, too.

At the scaffold, where he was to die, St. Thomas kissed his executioner on the cheek. Then he joked, saying that his beard should not be cut off because it had not done anything wrong. He was martyred on Tuesday, July 6, 1535, at the age of fifty-seven. Along with his friend, Bishop John Fisher, Sir Thomas More was proclaimed a saint by Pope Pius XI in 1935.

This saint is universally admired because he believed so much in the truth of his faith that he was willing to die for it. Thomas More risked losing everything: his fortune, his position, his own security and the safety of the individuals he loved most. But he held fast to the faith, even to the point of sacrificing his life. He makes us ask ourselves what we might do in a similar situation.

ST. JOSEPH CAFASSO

Joseph Cafasso was born in 1811, in northern Italy, near the city of Turin. Four years later, in 1815, one of his most famous students was born in the same town, St. John Bosco. We celebrate his feast on January 31. Joseph had loving parents who were willing to sacrifice for his education. He went to Turin to study to become a priest.

Joseph met John Bosco in 1827 when Bosco was twelve. He talked to Seminarian Cafasso at the church and ran all the way home. "Mom, Mom," John called, "I met him, I met him!" "Who?" his mother asked. "Joseph Cafasso, mother. He's a saint, I tell you." Mrs. Bosco smiled and nodded gently. In 1833, Joseph was ordained a priest. He began his priestly work and went to an excellent school of theology for priests. When Father Cafasso graduated, he became a theology professor. He taught many young priests over the years. They could tell that he really loved them.

Father Cafasso became known as the priest who believed in the gentle and loving mercy of God. Because he was so kind himself, he gave people courage and hope. He guided many priests, religious and lay people. He helped John Bosco begin his great priestly ministry with boys. He also guided Father Bosco in starting his religious order known as the Salesians. Father Cafasso directed other founders, too.

There were many social needs in Father Cafasso's time. One of the most urgent was the prison system. Prison conditions were disgusting. But what most moved Father Cafasso was the custom of hanging in public prisoners sentenced to death. Father Cafasso went to them and heard their confessions. He stayed with them, telling them of God's love and mercy until they died. He helped over sixty convicted men. All repented and died in the peace of Jesus. Father Cafasso called them his "hanged saints."

Father Cafasso also became the pastor of St. Francis Church in 1848. No one could ever measure his great influence on people and works in the Church. Father Cafasso died on June 23, 1860. His devoted friend, St. John Bosco, preached the homily at his funeral. Pope Pius XII proclaimed him a saint in 1947.

We can never be too kind and understanding with people. If we should be tempted to take others for granted, or just look after ourselves, we can pray to St. Joseph Cafasso. He will help us to become "big-hearted" like he was.

THE BIRTH OF JOHN THE BAPTIST

John's parents were Zachary and Elizabeth. Elizabeth was a cousin of Mary, the mother of Jesus. Mary went to visit and help when Elizabeth was old and about to become a mother.

St. Elizabeth had her baby. Zachary named him John, as the angel had requested. John had a special calling. He was going to prepare the way for the coming of Jesus. So when he was still young, he went into the desert to prepare himself with silence, prayer and penance. Soon crowds started to come to him. They realized he was a holy man. He warned them to be sorry for their sins. He told them to change their lives, and he gave them the baptism of repentance. One day, Jesus himself came to John. He wanted to be baptized with John's baptism to begin making up for our sins. On that day, John told the crowds that Jesus was the Messiah, the one they had been waiting for. He told them and everyone else to follow him.

Later on, St. John learned that King Herod had married a woman who already had a husband and a daughter. This king was the son of the King Herod who had murdered all those little boys in Bethlehem. St. John told him that it was wrong for him to live with that woman. King Herod was angry and humiliated. He locked John up in prison. John remained in a dark, damp dungeon until Herod had him killed.

St. John's motto was, "Jesus must become more and more. I must become less and less." He said that he was not even worthy to loosen the strap of Jesus' sandal.

John the Baptist was a great prophet. Chapter eleven of Matthew's Gospel praises him in the words of Jesus himself. When we want to be "number one," we can ask St. John the Baptist to teach us how to be humble. We can ask him also to help us realize the value of being humble.

JUNE 25

ST. WILLIAM OF MONTE VERGINE

William was born in Vercelli, Italy, in 1085. His parents died when he was a baby. Relatives raised him. When William grew up, he became a hermit. He worked a miracle, curing a blind man, and found himself famous. William was too humble to be happy with the people's admiration. He really wanted to remain a hermit so that he could concentrate on God. He went away to live alone on a high, wild mountain. No one would bother him now. But even there he was not to remain alone. Men gathered around the saint and they built a monastery dedicated to the Blessed Virgin. Because of William's monastery, people gave the mountain a new name. They called it the Mountain of the Virgin.

After a while, some of the monks began to complain that the lifestyle was too hard. They wanted better food and an easier schedule. William would not relax the rule for himself. Instead, he chose a prior for the monks. Then he and five faithful followers set out to start another monastery, as strict as they were used to. One of his companions was St. John of Mantua. Both William and John of Mantua were leaders. They realized as time went on that they would do better if they split up, each to start a monastery. They were great friends, but they saw things differently. John went east and William went west. Both did very well. In fact, both became saints.

Later, King Roger of Naples helped St. William. William's good influence on the king angered some evil men of the court. They tried to prove to the king that William was really evil, that he was hiding behind a holy habit. They sent a bad woman to tempt him, but she was unsuccessful. It seems that she repented and gave up her life of sin.

St. William died on June 25, 1142.

If you have trouble getting along with someone or liking someone, just ask St. William to show you the good in that person. He will inspire you to know how to become friends with that person.

ST. PELAGIUS

This boy martyr of Spain lived in the days when the Moors ruled part of his homeland. The Moors were fighting the Spanish Christians. Pelagius was only ten when his uncle had to leave him as a hostage with the Moors in the city of Cordova. He would not be allowed to go free until his uncle sent him what the Moors demanded.

Three years passed and still the young Christian remained a prisoner. By this time, he was a handsome, lively boy of thirteen. Although many of his fellow prisoners were men who had acquired evil habits, Pelagius would not imitate their example. Even though he was young, he had a strong will and knew how to keep himself good.

The ruler of the Moors heard good reports about Pelagius. He sent for the boy. Pelagius was handsome and well-behaved. The ruler felt generous and wanted to get him out of prison. After all, he was only a boy. Pelagius was offered his freedom, plus fine clothes to wear. Not only that, he would receive beautiful horses and money. All of these would be his if he would give up his faith and become a Muslim like his captors.

"All those things you named mean nothing to me," answered the boy firmly. "I have been a Christian. I am a Christian now. I shall continue to be a Christian." The ruler was surprised. He changed his approach. Instead of promises came threats, but none had any effect.

Thirteen-year-old Pelagius died a martyr in the year 925.

Pelagius reminds us that our commitment to Christ is serious and has consequences in our daily lives. When we find ourselves weakening, unable to withstand peer pressure, we can ask St. Pelagius to make us as strong and mature in our faith as he was.

JUNE 27

ST. CYRIL OF ALEXANDRIA

Cyril was born in Alexandria, Egypt, in 370. His uncle, Theophilus, was the patriarch or archbishop. His uncle meant well, but he had a bad temper and could be stubborn at times. He couldn't have known, as we do, that the famous John Chrysostom would be a saint some day. We celebrate St. John Chrysostom's feast on September 13. Archbishop Theophilus was responsible for sending John into exile in 403. But the emperor brought the famous bishop back to his archdiocese of Constantinople. It seems that Cyril was influenced by his uncle's prejudice of John, and agreed when he was sent into exile.

When his uncle died in 412, Cyril became the archbishop. He was very clear about his love for the Church and for Jesus. He was a brave man in confusing times and preached what the Church taught. He was honest and straightforward. He was not looking for praise or positions. However, Cyril could be impulsive and stubborn at times. He wanted to express the truths of the Church with his preaching and writing, and he did. But when he became upset, what he said was not always easy to follow. Of course, he was not concerned about saying things in a gentle way, so he blurted out angrily at times.

This must have caused him sorrow. Yet Christians were grateful for his many wonderful qualities. For example, he was not afraid to defend the Church and what we believe.

St. Cyril was the representative of Pope St. Celestine I at the Council of Ephesus in 431. This was an official Church meeting of over two hundred bishops. They had to study the teachings of a priest named Nestorius. The Council explained clearly that Nestorius was wrong about some important truths we believe. The pope gave him ten days to say he would not keep preaching his mistakes. But Nestorius would not give in. The Council explained to the people of God that we could not accept the mistakes. The bishops were so clear in their explanation that these false teachings would never again be a major threat.

The people were very grateful to St. Cyril of Alexandria who led the Council meetings. Nestorius went quietly back to his monastery and stopped confusing people. Cyril went back to his archdiocese and worked hard for the Church until he died in 444. Pope Leo XIII proclaimed St. Cyril a Doctor of the Church in 1883.

It doesn't pay to become discouraged when we don't perform as well as we should. We can pray to St. Cyril and ask him to help us live with our limitations.

JUNE 28

ST. IRENAEUS

Irenaeus was a Greek who was born between the years 120 and 140. He had the great privilege of being taught by St. Polycarp, who had been a disciple of St. John the Apostle. Irenaeus once told a friend: "I listened to St. Polycarp's instructions very carefully. I wrote down his actions and his words, not on paper, but on my heart."

After he became a priest, Irenaeus was sent to the French city of Lyons. It was in this city that the bishop, St. Pothinius, was martyred along with a great many other saints. Irenaeus was not martyred at that time because he was asked by his brother priests to take an important message from them to the pope in Rome. In that letter they spoke of Irenaeus as a man full of zeal for the faith.

When Irenaeus returned to be the bishop of Lyons, the persecution was over. But there was another danger: a heresy called Gnosticism. This false religion attracted some people by its promise to teach them secret mysteries. Irenaeus studied all its teachings and then in five books showed how wrong they were. He wrote with politeness, because he wanted to win people to Jesus. However, sometimes his words were strong, such as when he said: "As soon as a man has been won over to the Gnostics, he becomes puffed up with conceit and self-importance. He has the majestic air of a rooster who goes strutting about." St. Irenaeus' books were read by many people. Before too long, the whole heresy began to die out. St. Irenaeus died around the year 202. Many believe he was martyred.

St. Irenaeus always remembered what he had been taught by St. Polycarp. We, too, can form the habit of being grateful to those who have taught us many good things. We can try to put what we have learned into practice. We can also pray for those who have taught us.

JUNE 29

ST. PETER AND ST. PAUL

St. Peter

Peter, the first pope, was a fisherman from Galilee. Jesus invited him to follow him, saying: "I will make you a fisher of men." Peter was a simple, hard-working man. He was generous, honest and very attached to Jesus.

This great apostle's name was Simon, but Jesus changed it to Peter, which means "rock." "You are Peter," Jesus said, "and on this rock I will build my Church." Peter was the chief or prince of the apostles.

When Jesus was arrested, Peter became afraid. It was then that he committed the sin of denying Our Lord three times. Fear for his safety got the best of him. But Peter repented totally. He wept over his denials for the rest of his life. Jesus forgave Peter. After his resurrection he asked Peter three times: "Do you love me?" "Lord," Peter answered, "you know all things. You know that I love you." Jesus truly did know! Peter was so right. Jesus said kindly: "Feed my lambs. Feed my sheep." He was telling Peter to take care of his Church because he would be ascending into heaven. Jesus left Peter as the leader of his followers.

Peter eventually went to Rome to live. Rome was the center of the whole Roman Empire. Peter converted many nonbelievers there. When the fierce persecution of Christians began, they begged Peter to leave Rome and save himself. It is said that he actually started out. On the road he met Jesus. Peter asked him, "Lord, where are you going?" Jesus answered, "I am coming to be crucified a second time." Then St. Peter turned around and went back. He realized that this vision meant that he was to suffer and die for Jesus. Soon after, he was taken prisoner and condemned to death. Because he was not a Roman citizen, he, like Jesus, could be crucified. This time he did not deny the Lord. This time he was ready to die for him. Peter asked to be crucified with his head downward since he was not worthy to suffer as Jesus had. The Roman soldiers did not find this unusual because slaves were crucified in the same manner.

St. Peter was martyred on Vatican Hill. It was around the year 67. Emperor Constantine built a large church over that sacred location in the fourth century. Recent archaeological findings confirm these facts.

We can learn from St. Peter that when we make Jesus the center of our hearts and our lives, everything else will work out.

St. Paul

Paul is the great apostle who first persecuted the Christians. Then he was converted. We celebrate Paul's conversion on January 25. At the time of his conversion, Jesus had said: "I will show him how much he must suffer for me." St. Paul loved Jesus very much, so much, in fact, that he became a living copy of our Savior. All his life, during his many missionary trips, St. Paul met troubles and went through dangers of every kind. He was whipped, stoned, shipwrecked, and lost at sea. Many, many times he was hungry, thirsty and cold.

Yet he always trusted in God. He never stopped preaching. "The love of Jesus presses me onward," he said. In reward, God gave him great comfort and joy in spite of every suffering.

We read about his marvelous adventures for Christ in Luke's Acts of the Apostles, beginning with chapter nine. But St. Luke's story ends when Paul arrives in Rome. He is under house arrest, waiting to be tried by Emperor Nero. A famous early Christian writer, Tertullian, tells us that Paul was freed after his first trial. But then he was put in prison again. This time he was sentenced to death. He died around the year 67, during Nero's terrible persecution of the Christians.

Paul called himself the apostle of the Gentiles. He preached the Gospel to the non-Jews. That took him to the whole known world. Because of Paul, we, too, have received the Christian faith.

Sometimes we realize that our faith is not strong enough. It is then that we can pray to St. Paul. He will help us believe in and love Jesus as he did.

꧁

JUNE 30

FIRST MARTYRS OF THE CHURCH OF ROME

The people we honor today had one thing in common: they gave up their lives for Christ. They were martyred because they were followers of the Lord Jesus. By the year 64, Emperor Nero's human rights violations had reached proportions beyond description. When a fire broke out in Rome on July 16, it was commonly believed that the emperor himself was responsible. As two-thirds of Rome lay in ruin, resentment grew. Nero became fearful. He needed a scapegoat and blamed the fire on the Christians.

Tacitus, a well-known historian, recorded that the Christians suffered cruel deaths. Some were fed to wild beasts. Others were tied to posts and became human torches that lit the Roman streets. The exact number of heroes is not known, but their gift of witness and their lives made a lasting impact on the people. Nero's was the first persecution by a Roman emperor, but not the last. And the more the Church was persecuted, the more it grew. The martyrs had paid the price so that all who would come after them could have the opportunity to embrace the faith.

We can pray to the martyrs of Rome for the courage to be true to what our Church teaches. These martyrs remind us, too, that we should seriously study our faith and read good Catholic books.

INDEX

*Alphabetical Listing by First Name of the Saints
In Volumes I and II*

A

St. Andrew Fournet - May 13

St. Andrew Kim Taegon and St. Paul Chong Hasang - September 20 (volume 2)

St. Angela Merici - January 27

St. Anne and St. Joachim - July 26 (volume 2)
St. Anne: patroness of Canada, of mothers, grandmothers, homemakers, and of cabinet-makers

Bl. Anne of St. Bartholomew - June 7

Annunciation of the Lord - March 25

St. Anselm - April 21

St. Anthony Claret - October 24 (volume 2)

St. Anthony Mary Zaccaria - July 5 (volume 2)

Bl. Anthony Neyrot - April 10

St. Anthony of Egypt - January 17
patron of grave diggers, butchers, basket and brush makers

St. Anthony of Padua - June 13
patron of finding lost articles, of the poor, of childless married women, of cemetery workers

St. Antoninus - May 10

St. Anysia - December 30 (volume 2)

St. Apollonia and the Martyrs of Alexandria - February 9
patroness of dentists and prayed to for tooth aches

Assumption of the Blessed Virgin Mary - August 15 (volume 2)

St. Athanasius - May 2

St. Augustine - August 28 (volume 2)
patron of theologians, printers and brewers

St. Augustine of Canterbury - May 27
patron of England

B

St. Barachisius and St. Jonas - March 29

St. Barbatus - February 19

St. Barnabas - June 11
patron of Antioch

St. Bartholomew - August 24 (volume 2)
patron of plasterers

St. Basil and St. Gregory Nazianzen - January 2
St. Basil: patron of hospital administrators

St. Basilissa and St. Julian - January 9

St. Bathildis - January 30

Venerable Bede - May 25

Beheading of St. John the Baptist - August 29
(volume 2)

St. Benedict - July 11 (volume 2)
*co-patron of Europe with St. Cyril and St. Methodius,
patron of monks and protector against poisoning*

St. Benedict Joseph Labre - April 16
patron of homeless people

St. Berard and Companions - January 16

St. Bernadette - February 18
*patroness of victims of asthma and children of
alcoholic parents*

St. Bernard - August 20 (volume 2)
patron of candle makers

St. Bernardine of Siena - May 20
*patron of advertisers, media personnel; people in public
relations and prayed to by or for people addicted to
gambling*

St. Bertilla - November 5 (volume 2)

Bl. Bertrand - September 6 (volume 2)

St. Bibiana - December 2 (volume 2)

Birth of the Blessed Virgin Mary - September 8
(volume 2)

Birth of John the Baptist - June 24

St. Blase - February 3
patron and protector against throat ailments

St. Botvid - July 28 (volume 2)

St. Bonaventure - July 15 (volume 2)

St. Boniface - June 5
patron of Germany

St. Boris and St. Gleb - July 24 (volume 2)

St. Bridget of Sweden - July 23 (volume 2)
patroness of Sweden

St. Brigid of Ireland - February 1
patroness of Ireland, of newborn babies and of dairy workers

St. Bruno - October 6 (volume 2)
patron of priests who expel demons (exorcists)

C

St. Caesarius of Nazianzen - February 25

St. Caius and St. Soter - April 22

St. Cajetan - August 7 (volume 2)

St. Callistus I - October 14 (volume 2)

St. Canute - January 19

St. Casimir - March 4
patron of Poland

St. Catherine Laboure - November 28 (volume 2)

St. Catherine of Ricci - February 13

St. Catherine of Siena - April 29
patroness of Italy, of nurses and of fire prevention

St. Catherine of Alexandria - November 25 (volume 2)
patroness of philosophers, jurists, teachers, students, and wheel-makers

Bl. Catherine of St. Augustine - May 8

St. Cecilia - November 22 (volume 2)
patroness of musicians, of poets, singers and organ builders

St. Celestine V - May 19
patron of bookbinders

St. Chaeremon and St. Ischyrion - December 22 (volume 2)

Chair of St. Peter - February 22

St. Charbel - December 24 (volume 2)

St. Charles Borromeo - November 4 (volume 2)
patron of catechists

St. Charles Lwanga and Companions - June 3
   St. Charles Lwanga: patron of black African children
Bl. Charles the Good - March 2
Christmas, the Birthday of Jesus - December 25
   (volume 2)
Bl. Christina - January 18
St. Clare - August 11 (volume 2)
   patroness of television
St. Colette - March 6
St. Columban - November 23 (volume 2)
   patron of Ireland and Irish monks
Bl. Contardo Ferrini - October 27 (volume 2)
   patron of universities
Conversion of St. Paul - January 25
St. Cornelius and St. Cyprian - September 16
   (volume 2)
St. Cosmas and St. Damian - September 26 (volume 2)
   patrons of surgeons, barbers, doctors and pharmacists
St. Cuthbert - March 20
   patron of sailors
St. Cyril and St. Methodius - February 14
   co-patrons of Europe along with St. Benedict
St. Cyril of Alexandria - June 27
St. Cyril of Jerusalem - March 18

D

St. Damasus I - December 11 (volume 2)
Bl. Damien of Molokai - April 15
St. David I of Scotland - May 24
St. Denis and Companions - October 9 (volume 2)
St. Deogratias - March 22
Bl. Didacus - March 24
St. Dominic - August 8 (volume 2)
   patron of astronomers
St. Dominic of Silos - December 20 (volume 2)
St. Dominic Savio - March 9
   patron of choir boys

E

St. Eanswida - September 12 (volume 2)

St. Edmund - November 20 (volume 2)

St. Edmund Campion - December 1 (volume 2)

St. Edward - October 13 (volume 2)

Eleven Martyrs of Almeria, Spain - October 10 (volume 2)

St. Elizabeth Ann Seton - January 4

St. Elizabeth Bichier - August 26 (volume 2)

St. Elizabeth of Hungary - November 17 (volume 2)
patroness of third order members, of bakers, of soup kitchens and shelters

St. Elizabeth of Portugal - July 4 (volume 2)

St. Emily de Vialar - June 17

St. Ephrem - June 9

St. Eucherius - February 20

Bl. Eugene de Mazenod - May 21

Bl. Eugene III - July 8 (volume 2)

St. Eulogius of Spain - March 11

St. Euphrasia - March 13

St. Eusebius - August 2 (volume 2)

St. Evaristus - October 26 (volume 2)

F

St. Fabian and St. Sebastian - January 20

St. Faustina and St. Jovita - February 15
patrons of the city of Brescia

St. Felicity and St. Perpetua - March 7
St. Felicity: patroness of motherhood

St. Felicity and Her Seven Sons - July 10 (volume 2)

St. Felix and St. Cyprian - October 12 (volume 2)

St. Felix II - March 1

St. Fidelis of Sigmaringen - April 24

St. Fina (Seraphina) - March 12

First Martyrs of the Church of Rome - June 30

St. Flannan - December 18 (volume 2)

St. Flora of Beaulieu - October 5 (volume 2)

St. Foillan - October 31 (volume 2)

St. Frances of Rome - March 9
patroness of motorists along with St. Christopher

Bl. Francis Anthony of Lucera - November 29

St. Francis Caracciolo - June 4

St. Francis de Sales - January 24
patron of authors, journalists and deaf people

St. Frances Xavier Cabrini - November 13 (volume 2)
patroness of immigrants, emigrants and hospital administrators

St. Francis of Assisi - October 4 (volume 2)
patron of Italy, of Catholic Action, of merchants, ecologists and animals

St. Francis of Paola - April 2
patron of seamen

St. Francis Xavier - December 3 (volume 2)
patron of missionaries, of the Apostleship of Prayer, of Borneo, Australia, New Zealand and China

Bl. Francois de Montmorency Laval - May 6

Bl. Frederic Janssoone - August 5 (volume 2)

St. Frederick - July 18 (volume 2)

G

St. Gabriel, St. Michael and St. Raphael - September 29 (volume 2)
St. Gabriel: patron of radio, television, telephone workers and mail carriers

St. Gabriel of Our Lady of Sorrows - February 27
patron of seminarians and youth

St. Genevieve - January 3
patroness of Paris

St. George - April 23
patron of England, of soldiers, of farmers and of Boy Scouts

St. Gerard of Brogne - October 3 (volume 2)

St. Germaine of Pibrac - June 15
patroness of sheep herders

St. Gertrude - November 16 (volume 2)
patroness of the West Indies

St. Gildas - January 29

St. Giles - September 1 (volume 2)
patron of crippled people, homeless people and blacksmiths

Bl. Giles Mary - February 7

St. Godfrey - November 8 (volume 2)

Bl. Gregory Barbarigo - June 18

St. Gregory Nazianzen and St. Basil the Great - January 2

St. Gregory the Great - September 3 (volume 2)
patron of England and of teachers

St. Gregory VII - May 25

Guardian Angels - October 2 (volume 2)

H

Bl Henry of Treviso - June 10

St. Henry II - July 13 (volume 2)
patron of Benedictine Oblates

St. Hilarion - October 21 (volume 2)

St. Hilary of Poitiers - January 13
patron and protector against snake bites

St. Hippolytus and St. Pontian - August 13 (volume 2)

The Holy Innocents - December 28 (volume 2)

St. Hugh of Grenoble - April 1

I

St. Ignatius of Antioch - October 17 (volume 2)

St. Ignatius of Laconi - May 11

St. Ignatius of Loyola - July 31 (volume 2)
patron of retreats and of soldiers

Immaculate Conception of Mary - December 8
(volume 2)

St. Irenaeus - June 28

St. Isaac Jogues, St. John de Brebeuf and Companions-
October 19 (volume 2)

St. Isidore of Seville - April 4

St. Isidore the Farmer - May 15
patron of farmers

J

St. James the apostle - July 25 (volume 2)
*patron of pharmacists, pilgrims, victims of arthritis,
manual laborers, hat makers and patron of Spain and
Chile*

St. James and St. Philip - May 3

Bl. James Duckett - April 19

St. James Intercisus - November 27 (volume 2)

St. Jane Frances de Chantal - August 18 in USA
(volume 2)
patroness of hunters

St. Jane Valois - February 4

St. Januarius - September 19 (volume 2)
patron of blood banks

St. Jerome - September 30 (volume 2)
patron of librarians

St. Jerome Emiliani - February 8
patron of orphans and homeless children

St. Joachim and St. Anne - July 26 (volume 2)
St. Joachim: patron of grandfathers

Bl. Joan Delanoe - August 17 (volume 2)

St. Joan of Arc - May 30
patron of France, of virgins, service women and soldiers

Bl. Joan of Toulouse - March 31

St. John Baptist de la Salle - April 7
patron of teachers

St. John Baptist Rossi - May 23

St. John Berchmans - November 26 (volume 2)
patron of students and altar boys

St. John Bosco - January 31
patron of editors and of laborers

St. John Capistrano - October 23 (volume 2)
patron of jurists and military chaplains

St. John Chrysostom - September 13 (volume 2)
patron of preachers

St. John Climacus - March 30

St. John Damascene - December 4 (volume 2)

St. John de Brebeuf, St. Isaac Jogues and Companions-
October 19 (volume 2)

Bl. John Duckett and Bl. Ralph Corby - September 7
(volume 2)

St. John DuLac and the September Martyrs -
September 2 (volume 2)

St. John Eudes - August 19 (volume 2)

St. John Fisher and St. Thomas More - June 22

St. John Francis Regis - June 16
patron of medical social workers

St. John I - May 18

St. John Gaulbert - July 12 (volume 2)
patron of forest workers

St. John Kanty - December 23 (volume 2)

St. John Joseph of the Cross - March 5

St. John Leonardi - October 9 (volume 2)

St. John Neumann - January 5

St. John of Egypt - March 27

St. John of God - March 8
*patron of hospitals, of the sick, of heart patients, of
nurses and of book sellers*

Bl. John of Rieti - August 9 (volume 2)

St. John of Sahagun - June 12

St. John of the Cross - December 14 (volume 2)

St. John Roberts - December 10 (volume 2)

St. John the Almsgiver - January 23

St. John the Apostle - December 27 (volume 2)
patron of Asia Minor

St. John Vianney - August 4 (volume 2)
patron of parish priests

St. Jonas and St. Barachisius - March 29

St. Josaphat - November 12 (volume 2)

St. Joseph - March 19
patron of the Universal Church, of the dying, of families, of carpenters, of providing for spiritual and physical needs

St. Joseph the Worker - May 1
patron of workers

St. Joseph Barsabbas - July 20 (volume 2)

St. Joseph Cafasso - June 23
patron of prisoners

St. Joseph Calasanz - August 25 (volume 2)
patron of Christian schools

St. Joseph Cupertino - September 18 (volume 2)
patron of aviators

St. Joseph Moscati - April 12

St. Jovita and St. Faustinus - February 15
patrons of the city of Brescia

Bl. Juan Diego - December 9 (volume 2)

St. Jude and St. Simon - October 28 (volume 2)
St. Jude: patron of impossible, desperate cases and of hospitals

St. Judith of Prussia - May 5

St. Julian and St. Basilissa - January 9

St. Julie Billiart - April 8

Bl. Junipero Serra - July 1 (volume 2)

St. Justin - June 1
patron of philosophers

K

Bl. Kateri Tekakwitha - July 14 (volume 2)
patroness of Native Americans

Bl. Katharine Drexel - March 3

St. Kenneth - October 11 (volume 2)

L

Bl. Lawrence Humphrey, Bl. Roger Dickenson, Bl. Ralph Milner - July 7 (volume 2)

St. Lawrence - August 10 (volume 2)
patron of cooks and the poor

St. Lawrence Brindisi - July 21 (volume 2)

St. Lawrence Justinian - September 5 (volume 2)

St. Lawrence O'Toole - November 14 (volume 2)

St. Lawrence Ruiz and Companions - September 28 (volume 2)

St. Leo IV - July 17 (volume 2)

St. Leo the Great - November 10 (volume 2)

Bl. Lidwina - April 14
patroness of skaters

St. Louis of France - August 25 (volume 2)
patron of third order members and of barbers

Bl. Louis of Thuringia - September 11 (volume 2)

St. Lucius, St. Montanus and Companions - February 24

St. Lucy - December 13 (volume 2)
patroness of people with eye diseases

St. Ludger - March 26

St. Luke - October 18 (volume 2)
patron of medical doctors, painters, glass-workers and brewers

St. Lupicinus and St. Romanus - February 28

M

St. Macrina - January 14

St. Marcellinus and St. Peter - June 2

Bl. Margaret Pole - May 28

St. Margaret Mary - October 16 (volume 2)
apostle of the Sacred Heart

St. Margaret of Scotland - November 16 (volume 2)
patroness of learning

St. Marguerite Bourgeoys - January 12

Bl. Marguerite D'Youville - December 23 (volume 2)

St. Maria Goretti - July 6 (volume 2)
patroness of virgins, of chastity and of the Children of Mary

Bl. Marie-Leonie Paradis - May 4

Bl. Marie Rose Durocher - October 6 (volume 2)

St. Mark the Evangelist - April 25
patron of notaries

St. Martha - July 29 (volume 2)
patroness of cooks, domestic servants, hospital dietitians and inn keepers

St. Martin de Porres - November 3 (volume 2)
patron of Black Americans and hair dressers

St. Martin I - April 13

St. Martin of Tours - November 11 (volume 2)
patron of the homeless and of soldiers

Martyrs of Orange - July 9 (volume 2)

St. Mary Magdalene - July 22 (volume 2)

St. Mary Magdalen de Pazzi - May 25

Bl. Mary of the Incarnation - April 18

Mary, Mother of God - January 1

Mary, our Queen - August 22 (volume 2)

St. Matthew - September 21 (volume 2)
patron of bankers, tax collectors and accountants

St. Matilda - March 14

St. Matthias - May 14

St. Maximilian Kolbe - August 14 (volume 2)

St. Maximinius - May 29

St. Meletius - February 12

St. Methodius and St. Cyril - February 14

St. Methodius I- June 14

St. Michael, St. Gabriel, St. Raphael - September 29 (volume 2)

St. Michael: patron of France, of radiologists, of persons in battle, of paratroopers, of grocers, of mariners and helper in temptation

Bl. Michelina - June 20

Bl. Miguel Augustin Pro - November 23 (volume 2)

St. Monica - August 27 (volume 2)
patroness of mothers and converts

St. Montanus, St. Lucius and Companions - February 24

N

St. Narcissus - October 29 (volume 2)

St. Nereus and Achilleus - May 12

St. Nersus - November 19 (volume 2)

St. Nicholas - December 6 (volume 2)
patron of children, of sailors, of bakers, of merchants, of prisoners, of Greece and co-patron with St. Andrew of Russia

Bl. Nicholas Albergati - May 9

St. Nicholas Tolentino - September 10 (volume 2)
patron of mariners

St. Nino - December 15 (volume 2)

St. Norbert - June 6

Bl. Notker - April 6

O

St. Olympias - December 17 (volume 2)

St. Onesimus - February 16

St. Otto - July 2 (volume 2)

Our Lady of Guadalupe - December 12 (volume 2)
patroness of Mexico, Latin America and the Philippines

Our Lady of Lourdes - February 11

Our Lady of Mount Carmel - July 16 (volume 2)

Our Lady of Sorrows - September 15 (volume 2)

Our Lady of the Holy Rosary - October 7 (volume 2)

P/Q

St. Pacificus - September 24 (volume 2)

St. Pammachius - August 30 (volume 2)

St. Pancras - May 12

St. Pantaleon - July 27 (volume 2)
patron of doctors

St. Paschal Baylon - May 17
patron of Eucharistic congresses and Eucharistic societies

St. Patrick - March 17
patron of Ireland

St. Paul - January 25/June 29
patron of Malta, of journalists and of hospital public relations

Conversion of - January 25

St. Paul and St. Peter - June 29 (volume 2)

St. Paulinus of Nola - June 22

St. Paul Miki and Companions - February 6

St. Paul of the Cross - October 19 (volume 2)

St. Paul the Hermit - January 15
patron of weavers

St. Pelagius - June 26

St. Perpetua and St. Felicity - March 7

St. Peter and St. Marcellinus- June 2

St. Peter and St. Paul - June 29
St. Peter: patron of fishermen

St. Peter Canisius - December 21 (volume 2)
patron of Germany

St. Peter Chanel - April 28

St. Peter Claver - September 9 (volume 2)
patron of Colombia and of Black Catholic missions

St. Peter Damian - February 21

St. Peter Julian Eymard - August 3 (volume 2)

St. Philip and St. James - May 3

St. Philip Neri - May 26
patron of Rome and of teenagers

St. Pius V - April 30

St. Pius X - August 21 (volume 2)

St. Polycarp - February 23

St. Pontian and St. Hippolytus - August 13 (volume 2)

St. Porcarius and Companions - August 12 (volume 2)

St. Porphyry - February 26

Presentation of Mary - November 21 (volume 2)

Presentation of the Lord - February 2

R

St. Radbertus - April 26

Bl. Ralph Corby and Bl. John Duckett - September 7 (volume 2)

St. Raphael, St. Michael and St. Gabriel - September 29 (volume 2)
St. Raphael: patron of blind people, of doctors, nurses, lovers, travelers and of happy endings

St. Raymond of Penyafort - January 7
patron of Church lawyers and of librarians of medical records

Bl. Richard Gwyn - October 25 (volume 2)

St. Richard of Chichester - April 3

St. Rita of Cascia - May 22
patroness of impossible cases

St. Robert Bellarmine - September 17 (volume 2)
patron of catechists

Bl. Roger Dickenson, Bl. Ralph Milner, Bl. Lawrence Humphrey - July 7 (volume 2)

St. Romanus and Lupicinus - February 28

St. Romuald - June 19

St. Rose of Lima - August 23 (volume 2)
patroness of the Americas, the Philippines and the West Indies

St. Rose of Viterbo - September 4 (volume 2)

St. Rose Philippine Duchesne - November 18 (volume 2)

Bl. Rose Venerini - May 7

S

St. Sabas - December 5 (volume 2)

St. Scholastica - February 10
patroness and protector against convulsions in children

St. Sebastian - January 20
patron of athletes and archers

St. Serapion - March 21

St. Sergius - September 25 (volume 2)

Seven Holy Founders of the Servite Order - February 17

St. Simeon - October 8 (volume 2)

St. Simon and St. Jude - October 28 (volume 2)

St. Simplicius - March 10

St. Sixtus II and Companions - August 7 (volume 2)

St. Soter and St. Caius - April 22

St. Stanislaus - April 11
patron of Poland and of receiving the Anointing of the Sick

St. Stephen - December 26 (volume 2)
patron of stonemasons and bricklayers

St. Stephen Harding - April 17

St. Stephen of Hungary - August 16 (volume 2)
patron of Hungary

St. Sylvester I - December 31 (volume 2)

T

St. Teresa of Avila - October 15 (volume 2)
protector against headaches

St. Thecla - September 23 (volume 2)

St. Theodore Tiro - November 9 (volume 2)

St. Theodosius - January 11

St. Theophane Venard - November 6 (volume 2)

St. Theresa of the Child Jesus - October 1 (volume 2)
patroness of missionaries, of tuberculosis patients, of aviators and of florists

St. Thomas - July 3 (volume 2)
patron of the East Indies and of architects

St. Thomas Aquinas - January 28
universal patron of universities, colleges and schools

St. Thomas Becket - January 29 (volume 2)

St. Thomas More and St. John Fisher - June 22
St. Thomas More: patron of lawyers

St. Thomas of Villanova - September 22 (volume 2)

St. Thorfinn - January 8

St. Timothy and St. Titus - January 26
St. Timothy: patron and protector against stomach disorders

Bl. Timothy Giaccardo - October 22 (volume 2)
patron of media evangelizers

St. Titus and St. Timothy - January 26
St. Titus: patron of Crete

Bl. Torello - March 16

The Transfiguration - August 6 (volume 2)

Triumph of the Holy Cross - September 14 (volume 2)

St. Turibius of Mongrovejo - March 23

St. Tutilo - March 28

U

St. Ubald - May 16

Bl. Urban V - December 19 (volume 2)

V

St. Vincent de Paul - September 27 (volume 2)
patron of charitable institutions

St. Vincent Ferrer - April 5
patron of builders

St. Vincent of Saragossa - January 22
  patron of wine growers
Visitation of Mary - May 31

W

St. Waldetrudis - April 9
St. William - January 10
St. William of Monte Vergine - June 25
St. William of York - June 28
St. Willibrord (volume 2) - November 7 (volume 2)
  patron of Holland and of epileptics

X/Y/Z

St. Zachary - March 15
St. Zita - April 27
  patroness of housekeepers and maids

Pauline BOOKS & MEDIA

CALIFORNIA
3908 Sepulveda Blvd., Culver City, CA 90230; 310-397-8676
5945 Balboa Ave., San Diego, CA 92111; 619-565-9181
46 Geary Street, San Francisco, CA 94108; 415-781-5180

FLORIDA
145 S.W. 107th Ave., Miami, FL 33174; 305-559-6715

HAWAII
1143 Bishop Street, Honolulu, HI 96813; 808-521-2731

ILLINOIS
172 North Michigan Ave., Chicago, IL 60601; 312-346-4228

LOUISIANA
4403 Veterans Memorial Blvd., Metairie, LA 70006; 504-887-7631

MASSACHUSETTS
50 St. Paul's Ave., Jamaica Plain, Boston, MA 02130; 617-522-8911
Rte. 1, 885 Providence Hwy., Dedham, MA 02026; 617-326-5385

MISSOURI
9804 Watson Rd., St. Louis, MO 63126; 314-965-3512

NEW JERSEY
561 U.S. Route 1, Wick Plaza, Edison, NJ 08817; 908-572-1200

NEW YORK
150 East 52nd Street, New York, NY 10022; 212-754-1110
78 Fort Place, Staten Island, NY 10301; 718-447-5071

OHIO
2105 Ontario Street, Cleveland, OH 44115; 216-621-9427

PENNSYLVANIA
9171-A Roosevelt Blvd., Philadelphia, PA
19114; 215-676-9494

SOUTH CAROLINA
243 King Street, Charleston, SC 29401; 803-577-0175

TENNESSEE
4811 Poplar Ave., Memphis, TN 38117; 901-761-2987

TEXAS
114 Main Plaza, San Antonio, TX 78205; 210-224-8101

VIRGINIA
1025 King Street, Alexandria, VA 22314; 703-549-3806

CANADA
3022 Dufferin Street, Toronto, Ontario, Canada M6B 3T5; 416-781-9131
1155 Yonge Street, Toronto, Ontario, Canada M4T 1W2; 416-934-3440